Thank You: You Are Already Making a Differenc

By purchasing this book, you've made a powerful choice. You're not only enriching your future, you're also helping others do the same.

Every dollar of profit from *Rich by Choice* goes directly to The Michels Family Corporation. It's a non-profit passionately committed to equipping and empowering others with the hand-ups they need to rise. Through education and unwavering support for those facing hardship, we strive to ignite potential and build pathways to brighter futures.

Because of you, children will learn how to dream bigger.
Because of you, families will gain tools to build a better tomorrow.
Because of you, lives will be changed.

From the bottom of our hearts, thank you. We are deeply grateful for your choice to join us. To learn more or explore ways to become more involved, please scan the QR code below or visit MichelsFamilyCorporation.com.

Together, we're helping others create a better future.

Thank you,
Nick and Chelsea Michels

"*Rich by Choice* is more than a financial guide; it's a blueprint for designing a life of purpose, freedom, and fulfillment. Nick's story is inspiring, his principles are practical, and his heart for helping others shines through every page. If you're ready to take control of your money and live life on your terms, this book is a must-read."

Justin Donald
#1 *Wall Street Journal* and *USA Today* Best-Selling Author, Founder of The Lifestyle Investor, Host of *The Lifestyle Investor* Podcast

RICH BY CHOICE

**TAKE BACK CONTROL, MASTER YOUR MONEY,
AND DESIGN THE LIFE OF YOUR DREAMS**

RICH BY CHOICE

TAKE BACK CONTROL, MASTER YOUR MONEY, AND DESIGN THE LIFE OF YOUR DREAMS

DR. NICHOLAS E. MICHELS

ethos
collective

Printed in the United States of America

Published by Igniting Souls
PO Box 43, Powell, OH 43065
IgnitingSouls.com

LCCN: 2024927516
Paperback ISBN: 978-1-63680-453-8
Hardcover ISBN: 978-1-63680-454-5
e-book ISBN: 978-1-63680-455-2

Available in paperback, hardcover, e-book, and audiobook.

Dedication

The Heart of My Story

To my beautiful wife, Chelsea—you are the love that fuels my soul, my greatest gift, and my best friend.

To my incredible children, Daegen Knox, Kinsley Blayke, Nicholas Brooks, and Everly Le'Ann—you are the light of my life, my greatest joy, and the legacy I am most proud to leave behind. This book is a reflection of all that you inspire in me.

Contents

Part I: Foundation

Part II: Fundamentals

Part III: Freedom

Foreword
by Dr. Kary Oberbrunner

Are You Ready to Take Back Control, Master Your Money, and Design the Life of Your Dreams?

Let's be honest, when we think about financial success, it's usually tied to how much money we have in the bank or how impressive our investment portfolio looks. But Dr. Nicholas E. Michels challenges us to think a little deeper. He asks, "Are you financially happy?" And that simple question flips the script. Suddenly, it's not just about chasing numbers; it's about building a life you actually love.

Dr. Nick has this rare ability to get people thinking—not just about money but about what truly matters. When he throws out questions like, *"When do you want to retire?"* or *"What does your ideal life actually cost?"* you can see the room shift. People start realizing that financial freedom isn't about stacking cash; it's about living with purpose.

That's exactly what *Rich by Choice* is all about. It's not a typical money book filled with recycled platitudes. It's a guide to figuring out what you want your life to look like and then using money as the tool to get you there. Nick walks you through a mindset shift from constantly chasing more to intentionally creating a life of meaning, balance, and freedom.

What's great is that this book isn't just for finance pros or seasoned investors. Whether you're just starting to think seriously about money or you're already on your way and want to sharpen your approach, Nick's got you covered. He breaks things down in a way that's practical and relatable, drawing from both years of experience and personal insight.

Inside, you'll learn how to build a strong financial foundation, make smart choices around earning and investing, and—most importantly—how to align your finances with your passions. Because at the end of the day, it's not just about wealth. It's about using money to live a life that feels rich in every sense of the word.

It's never too late to take control of your financial journey. And with *Rich by Choice* as your guide, you'll have everything you need to move forward with clarity, confidence, and purpose.

Let's dive in. Your path to financial happiness starts here.

Dr. Kary Oberbrunner
Wall Street Journal and *USA Today* bestselling author

Introduction

As I sat back, gazing out at a breathtaking view, I felt a surge of gratitude for the journey that had brought me here—the one that led me to write this book. It has been a lifetime of learning—through hardships, triumphs, and everything in between—the product of years of education, personal reflection, business success as a financial advisor, and faith that guided me through it all. At that moment, I had a brilliant idea for a book. A bit of anxiety crept in at the thought of sharing a book about my life and what I've learned. *How much time, effort, and money would it take to do that? What if no one resonated with my message?* Then, a curious question crept into my mind: *How much money would it take for me* not *to publish* Rich by Choice?

What would be your number? We all have a "number" in mind—a point where we might trade our time, energy, or even dreams for wealth. But here's the thing: *There is no number.* No amount of wealth, no temptation of luxury, could keep me from sharing what I've discovered. I've found something far more valuable than anything money can buy. It's like unearthing a hidden treasure, not of gold or jewels, but of peace, joy, and fulfillment.

The $8 Million Choice

How much is your integrity worth? Would you trade it for $8,131,500? It's a question that feels almost hypothetical. For me, it wasn't. It was real. And it came with a decision that would shape the course of my life.

I remember the moment like it was yesterday. At the time, I was soaring in my career as a financial advisor, a partner in a prestigious firm, with clients from all over the world entrusting me with their finances and their family's future. By every outward measure, I had made it. My career was everything I had worked for, a pinnacle of achievement. But inside, something wasn't right. There was a whisper, quiet at first but growing louder with each passing day—a gnawing feeling that something about the industry I loved was broken.

At first, it was subtle: an advisor suggesting a product that wasn't the best fit for a client, a firm's priority shifting ever so slightly toward its bottom line instead of the people it served. But those small cracks widened. The deeper I peered into the machinery of the financial world, the more I saw—and the less I could stomach. The system, I realized, wasn't built to serve families. Too often, it was designed to exploit them. Not every advisor or firm operated this way, of course, but the rot was undeniable. I began to see corruption, manipulation, and an alarming disregard for the trust clients placed in financial advisors and firms. It broke my heart. I had dedicated my life to helping people, and now I was questioning the very foundation of my work.

Then came the offer.

A competitor approached me with what seemed like the deal of a lifetime. They offered a signing bonus: $8,131,500. A life-changing number. To make it even sweeter, they promised my current salary would remain intact if I brought my clients over to their firm. On paper, it was an offer I couldn't refuse. But one question burned in my mind: *How could they afford to pay me so much?*

The answer was chillingly simple. They expected to earn far more from my clients in the years ahead—at my clients' expense. That realization stopped me cold. I couldn't unsee the truth. Saying yes would mean selling not just my integrity but the trust of every family who relied on me. I'd become part of the very system I could no longer believe in.

That night, I went home, heavy with the weight of the decision. My wife, my unwavering partner and greatest confidante, listened patiently as I spilled out my frustrations and fears. "I can't do this anymore," I told her. I think I need to quit and start something new—something better—a firm that truly puts people first."

Her response was simple and resolute: "Let's do it."

And so, we did. I turned down over $8 million, walked away from my position, and took a leap of faith into the unknown. Together, we built something entirely new: a financial firm rooted in trust, transparency, and care—a firm where families and their dreams come first, and profits are a byproduct of doing the right thing.

It wasn't easy. Starting from scratch rarely is. There were sleepless nights, hard conversations, and moments of doubt. But as we took each step forward, the nervousness gave way to clarity. We knew we had made the right choice. Today, our lives are richer than we could have ever imagined—and not just financially. We've found joy, peace, security, and a deep sense of purpose. We've created a life full of excitement, incredible memories, and, most importantly, happiness.

This isn't just about making more money, though, yes, that has come along the way. It's about transforming the way you live, love, and experience the world. Imagine waking up every day not burdened by stress or financial worries but filled with a deep sense of contentment, purpose, and abundance.

Here's the thing: *You have a choice too.*

This journey to become Rich by Choice has led me to a place where I no longer need anything more. I have all that I need, not because I'm content with material possessions, but because I've mastered the Fundamentals of Money—giving, saving, investing, earning, budgeting, planning, protecting, and spending wisely, all with a mindset of growth and gratitude.

The real magic happened when we realized the importance of integrating all these pillars into our lives. For too long, many of us have focused on just one or two areas while ignoring others, believing they weren't as critical, but financial peace and prosperity come from mastering the entire framework. This book is my story, woven with the stories of the many families I've had the privilege to help and the hard-earned lessons that led me to stumble upon the secrets of true wealth and happiness.

Let me be clear: I didn't start with all the answers. There was a time when my life was not what I envisioned. I faced struggles I couldn't explain and challenges I didn't understand. I did what most people in that situation would do: I set out to find the solutions I desperately needed. I devoured hundreds of books, pursued degrees from some of the most prestigious institutions, including Ivy League Schools, and interviewed over a thousand people from all walks of life. As I pieced together their stories and my own experiences, everything began to align. I discovered a path to financial happiness that is simple, powerful, and accessible to anyone.

What I found was *life-changing.* I began to understand the principles that drive true wealth—principles that transcend bank accounts and balance sheets. These principles shaped the fortunes of people worth millions, even hundreds of millions, and they're within your reach too. It's about aligning your finances with the life you want to live, with your relationships, your goals, and your sense of purpose.

How to Maximize This Book

Before we dive in, let me share a few suggestions on how to maximize this book. Think of me as your guide, money mentor, coach, and friend. I'm here to help you unlock the doors to the life you've always dreamed of living. You're not just reading a book; you're stepping into a partnership where my goal is to give you the tools and wisdom to create the life you deserve. Remember, this journey isn't just about money; it's about building a life that is rich in every sense of the word.

First and foremost, *be patient with yourself*. It's important to understand that it's *not your fault* if you feel overwhelmed by money. Despite how deeply money is woven into the fabric of our daily lives, most of us were never properly taught how to manage it. But that's exactly what we're here to change. Some of the concepts in this book may seem simple, yet they'll be new to you. You're not expected to become a financial expert overnight.

> Do not dwell on past mistakes; the would haves, should haves, or could haves won't help you.

Do not dwell on past mistakes; the would haves, should haves, or could haves won't help you. Every one of us has made errors along the way, myself included. What matters is that you're here now, ready to focus on your future. And trust me, it's a bright one. As Henry Ford once said, "Failure is simply the opportunity to begin again, this time more intelligently."

I did then what I knew how to do.
Now that I know better, I do better.

—Maya Angelou

Take your time with this book. *Read each chapter at least twice.* Repetition is the mother of all success. Don't just passively absorb the information; engage with it. Use a highlighter, take notes, write down the principles that stand out to you, and think about how they can improve your life. The more detailed and specific you get, the more powerful the transformation will be.

Consider these learning statistics from Jim Kwik, the author of *Limitless.*[1] We remember:

- 10 percent of what we read
- 20 percent of what we hear
- 30 percent of what we see
- 50 percent of what we see and hear
- 70 percent of what we say and write
- 90 percent of what we do

What does this mean? It means that the more active you are in this learning process, the faster the knowledge will stick with you and the deeper it will resonate. That's why this book includes activities, reflection questions, quizzes, and videos—so you can engage with the material in multiple ways and make it part of your life. Action fuels progress. As Tony Robbins says, "The path to success is to take massive, determined action."

The incredible impact of this book depends on you: the more you engage, the more your life will transform. Every moment you invest, every thought you direct, and every action you take will bring you closer to a life filled with greater wealth, peace, and happiness. The depth of your devotion to this journey will be reflected in the abundance you create. Embrace this fully, and you won't just read this book; you'll live its success. I want this book to give you the life you have always dreamed about.

The book's three sections are like the wheels of a tricycle; you need all three to keep moving forward. **Foundation** is about finding clarity in your life, defining your goals, and building the life you want for yourself and your family. **Fundamentals** explains the practical tools, strategies, and insights that will equip you to reach those goals. Finally, **Freedom** brings everything together. Individually, they are valuable; together, they are transformative.

Key Benefits

- **Build Wealth with Purpose While Boosting Confidence and Control:** Feel empowered through tools and insights that will grow your wealth intentionally with clarity, ensuring that every dollar you earn works toward your dreams and values.

- **Master the Art of Money and Unlock Financial Freedom:** Learn how to take control of your money, break free from paycheck-to-paycheck living, gain powerful insights into budgeting, investing, saving, and spending, and create the life you truly desire.

- **Experience Life on Your Terms and Design Your Dream Life:** Discover how to use money as a tool to fund adventures, experiences, and moments, and create a life filled with purpose, passion, and abundance by making intentional choices that align with your highest aspirations.

Here's my advice: Read one chapter a day. After each chapter, complete the exercise and reflect on how what you've just learned can apply to your life. Go to RichByChoiceBook.com/bonus or simply scan the QR code. Every word you read and exercise you complete is a step closer to being Rich by Choice, a place where your money, values, and dreams align perfectly.

This book isn't just about our journey. It's about yours. It's about the power of choosing to live a life of integrity, freedom, and joy. It's about finding your own path to financial happiness—a life of independence, peace, and fulfillment. The lessons in these pages are drawn from our story, but they are for *you*. They're here to help you take control of your finances, align them with your deepest values, and create a life that truly matters.

Right now, you're standing at the same crossroads I once faced. Being rich, happy, secure, and full of joy is not a matter of chance. It's a matter of *choice*. I made mine, and it changed everything. I am going to tell you my journey and show you how you can have an amazing life of financial happiness.

So, what will you choose?

This is your moment. Let me show you how to live a life of joy, peace, security, independence, excitement, unforgettable memories, and... happiness.

You can be *Rich by Choice*.

PART I

Foundation

1

Victor by Choice
Your Past and Present
Do Not Define You.

The last thing you want when picking up a book about improving your life is a long chapter about the author. This first chapter is deeply personal; it's about my journey, my struggles, overcoming hardships, the lessons I've learned, and the experiences that have shaped my passion for helping others. While your journey might be different from mine, I believe our stories have power, and this one might just inspire you in ways you don't expect.

But I also know that you may be here for the proven strategies, the tools, and the step-by-step guidance to create financial wealth and happiness in your own life. If that's the case, I completely understand—feel free to skip ahead to Chapter 2, where we'll jump right into "how to" become Rich by Choice. No matter where you begin, just know that this book was written for you, with the sole purpose of helping you build a life of wealth, joy, and purpose.

I stood frozen, the solid foundation of my life collapsing beneath me as terror and anxiety rushed in to fill the void. As I waited there, my heart began to pound faster and faster, as if it might burst from my chest. My palms were sweaty, my throat was tight, and my mind raced with questions. When the words "We're getting divorced" finally left their lips, everything inside me froze. I could feel the ground shifting beneath me, the world I thought I knew crumbling away as fear and confusion took over.

My life as I knew it was over. Those three words shattered the world I had known for the first ten years of my life. Everything would change—my family, my home, my sense of security. At that moment, I had no idea how deeply those words would shape my journey. I was just a kid, but the storm that was unleashed would turn my entire world upside down. Suddenly, my mom was all alone, raising four boys on her own.

We went from living in a large house in a nice neighborhood to squeezing into a small mobile home on the other side of town, where the only thing we had in abundance was the weight of our new reality. The life we had was gone, and it wasn't coming back.

It wasn't just the loss of material things that hurt; the emotional toll wore us down. I watched my mother, exhausted and burdened, doing everything she could to keep us afloat. My mom is my hero. She's incredible.

The financial hardships hit us like a tidal wave. Perhaps the hardest adjustment for my brothers and me was going

> **The only thing we had in abundance was the weight of our new reality.**

from having a stay-at-home mom to a single mom of four who had to work three jobs. Our entire lives changed—my entire universe changed. Our way of life had shattered.

As a child, I can vividly recall sitting in front of the TV, watching an old black-and-white cartoon. The episode was about a mother who worked tirelessly to prepare a special meal for her son. When the son asked for more, she had nothing left to give. She turned her face away in tears, heartbroken. That scene broke me. I still tear up thinking about it to this day. It mirrored the struggles my mom faced, trying to balance everything while the weight of the world rested on her shoulders.

It was at that moment, the crossroads of becoming aware of my life's current events and that specific cartoon, an idea awakened in me: *How much money greatly influences our lives...for good or for bad.* Money doesn't just impact your life; it shapes your happiness, your relationships, and your future. Master it, and you'll master the life you've always dreamed of. It's also about people wanting and trying to do the right thing, but not having the answers.

That's where my journey truly began. The hardships, the struggles, the emotional pain—all of it planted a seed in me.

I didn't want to see others go through what we had. I wanted to understand money, to master it, so that one day I could help others avoid the same pain. That drive, that passion to break free from financial struggle, became my guiding force.

Basketball: My Way Out

Amid the chaos and uncertainty, basketball became my refuge. It was more than just a game; it was my escape from the struggles at home and my way of carving out a future. When I stepped onto the court, everything else faded away. It was my sanctuary, the one place where I could control my fate. The hard work paid off, and I earned a basketball scholarship that opened the door to a world of higher education—an opportunity to rise above the hardship and rewrite my story.

The real lessons basketball taught me went far beyond the court. Early in my college years, I nearly flunked a class: Zoology. (It was a brutal class—and no, it wasn't a fun field trip with cuddly zoo animals like my naïve 18-year-old brain had hoped.) That was a turning point. I realized then that talent wasn't enough; I had to be disciplined, consistent, and committed—in academics and life. I developed a habit of studying during every free moment, even during commercial breaks while watching sports. That habit, those small, consistent efforts, became the foundation of my success. I went on to become a two-time All-American in basketball, but what truly fills me with pride is the academic journey that followed. I made the Dean's list multiple times, earned the honor of being a three-time Academic All-American, and was even named to *ESPN The Magazine*'s All-Academic Team—achievements beyond what I ever thought possible. The real lesson wasn't about basketball but life: *small, steady actions lead to big results.* It also taught me that the little things done consistently over time lead to massive success—no matter your background.

After college, I found myself living a dream I never expected: playing professional basketball in Europe. Travel-

Small, steady actions lead to big results.

ing the world while playing the game I loved felt like an incredible blessing. As a wide-eyed kid fresh out of school, I would've signed the first contract thrown my way—honestly, I would've played for free. My agent, likely wondering if I'd ever understand the concept of negotiation, had to remind me that playing for free wasn't a winning business strategy. But to me, the opportunity to explore new cultures, meet new people, and see the world was priceless.

One of the greatest lessons I took from that time was just how vast and beautiful this world truly is. We're all wonderfully different, and when you take the time to understand others and embrace those differences, you begin to see how much good there is in the world. A simple smile or act of kindness often gets returned in kindness—something I carry with me on and off the court. Traveling the world taught me that despite the challenges we face, there is far more good in people than we often realize.

The Internship: The Turning Point

Another pivotal chapter in my life came when I was required to complete an internship to graduate from Dallas Baptist University. I landed a spot with a family friend who was a financial advisor, and those six months would become one of the most transformative periods of my life. I fell in love with the work of helping people navigate their financial journeys, guiding them toward a secure and prosperous future. During this time, I met my first true mentor, a man whose devotion to his clients was as deep as his expertise in finance. He taught me a lesson that will stay with me for the rest of my life: *Always put others first*. His example showed me that success wasn't about making money; it was about making a difference.

I was young and eager, assuming my mentor's mindset was common in the financial world, but as I ventured further into my career, I quickly realized it wasn't. Many financial advisors and firms were focused on the bottom line, not on truly serving their clients. That contrast reinforced my commitment to building a career centered on integrity, compassion, and doing the right thing because when you do what's right for others, success naturally follows.

When you do what's right for others, success naturally follows.

From Victim to Victor

It would have been easy to let my early circumstances define me. Being a victim is easy. You *blame* your situation on your circumstances (my parents divorced), make *excuses* (my mom was busy working three jobs), and *deny* that you have a hand in changing your circumstances (I was just a kid). I chose not to lie in that BED.

Without consciously realizing it, I had thrown my OAR into the water. I took *ownership* of my life, held myself *accountable*, and acted *responsibly*. Was it easy? No. Has it been worth it? Yes. It's time for you to add the OAR to the financial waters and become Rich by Choice.

The OAR Reflection Exercise
(Ownership, Accountability, Responsibility)

Purpose: This exercise will help you identify areas where you may be stuck in a victim mindset and reframe your thinking toward ownership, accountability, and responsibility.[2]
Instructions:

- Take a moment to reflect on a financial or life challenge you're currently facing. Write it down.
- Now, ask yourself

    ○ Ownership: What part of this situation do I control?

    ○ Accountability: What actions (or inactions) have contributed to where I am today?

    ○ Responsibility: What is one step I can take today to change my circumstances?

- Write down an action step to shift from a victim to a victor mindset.

_____

_____

_____

If you are having trouble, do not worry. Reading this book is a very powerful action you are taking right now. Keep turning. One page at a time. Research states that when you take action, aka "Solution-Focused Thinking," it directs your attention away from the problem and expands your power for positive outcomes and peace of mind.

- Repeat this exercise anytime you catch yourself feeling powerless.

To download this exercise or explore other resources from this book, scan the QR code or visit RichByChoiceBook. com/bonus.

• • •

The choice to be a victor is only the first step, but it can be one of the most difficult. Everyone experiences struggles in their journey. It's the ones who decide to move beyond their circumstances who can move forward on the path of becoming Rich by Choice.

Nick and Chelsea Choose to be a Victor

Before my parents' divorce, my life was my mountain-top—a breathtaking peak where the air was crisp, the beautiful skies were endless, and every moment felt wrapped in peace, joy, security, and happiness. The views were mesmerizing, filled with vibrant dreams and the warmth of possibility, until life's unexpected storms sent me tumbling into a valley so dark and empty, it felt like the light had abandoned me. In that valley, I fought battles I didn't know I was strong enough to face, uncovering the secrets of resilience, growth, and transformation that became my ladder back to the summit. Now, my mission is clear: to help you find your way out of the valleys in your life and guide you to the beautiful heights you're destined to reach.

What's waiting for you when you climb out of the valley?

2

Empowerment by Choice
You Are More than a Statistic.

I t was a beautiful day when Jim and Lisa, a sweet couple in their early 60s, walked into my office. They had spent the last few decades building their business from the ground up. What started as a small idea between two newlyweds had blossomed into a thriving business that not only supported their family but also touched the lives of countless others. They were now ready to sell their beloved business and begin a new chapter, one filled with adventures around the world and precious time with their grandkids.

Jim and Lisa weren't just business owners; they were dreamers, workers, and doers. They had poured their hearts into every aspect of their business, always putting their customers first. With each passing year, their passion for serving people only grew stronger. From late nights to early mornings, from unexpected setbacks to triumphant successes, they built their legacy with determination and love.

Now, sitting in front of me, ready to talk about the sale of their business, their excitement was palpable. As they walked into the room, they immediately started rattling off numbers—dollars, cents, investment strategies, debt ratios, and business evaluations. They had spreadsheets, charts, and a plan for every penny. Jim's eyes sparkled as he discussed the intricacies of the sale, while Lisa, ever the detailed partner, nodded along, adding her own thoughts and ideas about their future finances.

As much as I appreciated their focus and thorough preparation, I couldn't help but smile. I could see that while their minds were buzzing with the technical details, their hearts were elsewhere, thinking about their future, their family, and their dreams. I needed to empower them to acknowledge those future thoughts. So, I gently interrupted their fast-paced conversation and said, "Hold on a minute. All of that is important, and we'll get to it; I promise. But first, let's talk about you. I care more about you and your family than your money."

They both paused, surprised, but then they smiled. At that moment, the weight of years of hard work and responsibility seemed to lift from their shoulders. Jim leaned back in his chair, and Lisa's eyes softened as she looked at him. They understood what

> "I care more about you and your family than your money."

I meant. Because, after all, numbers are just tools. Money, investments, and financial strategies are all essential but are not the end goal. The real goal is to use that money to protect and enhance what is most important to us: the people we love, the moments we cherish, and the lives we want to lead.

We spent the next several hours not discussing numbers but discussing life. Jim told me about his dreams of traveling to Italy, tasting wine in Tuscany, and finally having the time to read all the books he'd never gotten to. Lisa beamed as she shared her excitement about spoiling their grandchildren: creating memories filled with laughter, beach trips, and late-night storytelling by the fireplace. They talked about their family, their love for their children, and the joy of seeing their grandkids grow up.

As they shared their hopes for the future, I could see how important it was that their finances aligned with these dreams. It wasn't just about selling the business or maximizing their investments; it was about ensuring that the money they'd worked so hard for would provide the life they wanted. Their retirement wasn't just an end; it was a new beginning, a time to live freely, explore the world, and nurture the relationships that meant everything to them.

So, we got to work. Together, we created a plan that would empower them to maximize the sale of their business and retire with peace of mind. We made sure that their financial strategies would support not only their financial needs but also their emotional and personal goals. Jim and Lisa left my office that day with more than just a plan; they left with excitement and anticipation for the life that lay ahead of them.

In the end, it was never about the numbers. It was about their love for each other, their family, and the legacy they wanted to leave behind. I couldn't be happier to have played a part in helping them turn their dreams into reality.

That's what true financial planning is about: using money as a tool to protect and enhance what matters most... *to you*. Jim and Lisa's story reminds us all that while money is important, it's not the end goal. The real goal is a life well-lived, filled with love, purpose, and joy. And that, my friends, is the greatest goal of all: happiness. But sadly, most are not happy.

Personal Finance Is the Number One Cause of Stress in Our Lives

Despite this understanding, why do so many people struggle with unhappiness? If money is supposed to be a tool to better our lives, why does it often feel like the source of our stress and worry? We need to explore these questions to uncover the deeper issues at play.

In his book *Walden*, famous author Henry David Thoreau declares, "The mass of men leads lives of quiet desperation."[3] This quote reflects Thoreau's observation that many people go through life feeling trapped by the hardships of life and overwhelming stress, and often without experiencing true happiness. This raises an important question: What is the true state of financial well-being for most people here in America? Or what is the financial situation we face here in America that keeps so many from experiencing the fulfillment they seek?

In a nation bursting with opportunity and abundance, why do so many of us continue to feel the relentless grip of financial stress? Despite working tirelessly, earning a living, and striving for success, countless people find themselves buckling under the weight that money places on their lives. It's not just about keeping up with expenses; it's emotional exhaustion, the sleepless nights, and the strain it places on marriages and families. What was meant to be a tool for freedom and security has, for many, become a source of anxiety and conflict. How did we arrive at this point? In the midst of so much potential, why are we more weighed down by financial worry than empowered by it?

Money: A Life of Happiness or Stress

- According to research, 90% of Americans say **money causes them stress.**[4]
- While 70% say they are **experiencing extreme stress.**[5]
- Shockingly, 65% of Americans feel their **financial difficulties are so overwhelming** they don't know how to overcome them.[6]
- In America, 86% report that financial struggles have **worsened their mental health.**[7]
- Over 50% of Americans **lose sleep over money** concerns.[8]
- **Financial stress** is directly linked to:[9]

  - **Higher risks of depression and anxiety—** people struggling with debt are **twice as likely** to suffer from depression.
  - **Sleep disorders—**worrying about money keeps millions awake at night.
  - **Weight fluctuations—**financial stress leads to unhealthy eating patterns.
  - **Relationship difficulties—**money is the leading cause of fights in marriages.
  - **Physical health problems—**linked to headaches, high blood pressure, and even heart disease.
  - **Unhealthy coping mechanisms—**such as alcohol abuse, gambling, and overspending.

Money and Marriage Problems

- **Money is the number one cause of arguments in marriage** and a leading contributor to divorce.[10]
- Studies show that 94% of couples who say they have **a happy marriage** also say they **work together on their finances** and discuss their long-term financial goals.[11]
- Couples with **high levels of debt** and **poor communication** about finances are **twice as likely** to divorce.[12]
- **Eighty-six percent** of married couples **start their marriage in debt**, setting the stage for financial tension.[13]
- Those who describe their marriage as "great" are **twice as likely** to discuss money **daily or weekly** compared to those in struggling marriages.[14]
- **Half** of first marriages and **65 percent** of second marriages end in divorce, with financial struggles being a top reason.[15]

Retirement Problems

- Only 7% of American retirees have an **ideal level of income in retirement**.[16]
- Meanwhile, 40% of older Americans **rely solely on Social Security** for their retirement income.[17]
- Sadly, 81% of Americans don't know if they have enough money for retirement and **fear running out of money**.[18]

- **Nearly 70%** of Americans say their retirement plan is simply to **"keep working forever"** because they have no other option.[19]
- Sadly, 64% of Americans are expected to retire with **less than $10,000** saved. That's **207 million people** facing financial insecurity in retirement.[20]
- It has been reported that **46% of Americans who save for retirement** admit they are just **"guessing"** how much they'll need.[21]
- At least 30% of Americans **have no financial plan at all.**[22]
- Reportedly, 66% of **Millennials have nothing saved for retirement.**[23]
- While 70% of Millennials **don't contribute to their employer's retirement plan**, leaving free money on the table.[24]
- According to a study, 70% of Americans **don't have a will or estate plan**, meaning their families are left in financial chaos after they pass away.[25]

Money Education Problems

- The **lack of financial education costs Americans $415 billion** in 2020 alone.[26]
- One report found that 33% of Americans have **less than $5,000 saved for retirement.**[27]
- **$24 billion** in **free 401(k) matching contributions** went unclaimed in 2018.[28]
- **One in 5 Americans** saves **nothing**—spending every dollar they make.[29]

- Less than **25% of millennials** understand the basics of saving and budgeting.[30]
- Thanks to **social media and FOMO,** Americans feel **pressured to spend more** to keep up with a lifestyle they can't afford.[31]

Debt Problems

- **One in 3 Americans** has **more credit card debt than savings.**[32]
- **One in 3 Americans** only **pays the minimum** on their credit card balance each month, keeping them in long-term debt.[33]
- The average American carries **four credit cards,** adding to financial strain.[34]
- Americans pay a staggering **$104 billion per year** in credit card interest and fees, and this number grows by **10 percent annually.**[35]
- **Over 40% of student loan borrowers** are not making payments.[36]
- Studies show that 40% of Americans would have to **borrow money or cut essential expenses** to cover an unexpected bill.[37]
- More than half (52%) of Americans **struggle to make their mortgage payments.**[38]

Why This Matters

These statistics aren't just numbers; they represent millions of real people struggling under the weight of financial stress, debt, and lack of planning. The financial landscape is bleak for those who do nothing but transformative for those who take action.

Financial happiness is not a matter of income—it's a matter of *knowledge, discipline,* and *intentionality.* Those who take control of their money sleep better, have stronger marriages, retire with dignity, and build a life of purpose.

Life doesn't have to be this way. Your family doesn't have to be one of those statistics. You're probably thinking, "Well, of course, I don't want to be a statistic. But my finances are in terrible shape. I don't see a way out of it." The truth is that there is a way out, no matter who you are, where you live, what you do for a living, or your current financial state. You become Rich by Choice by using the principles, lessons, and guides in this book. Your life can be better. You can have the life you've always dreamed about.

> **Financial happiness is not a matter of income—it's a matter of *knowledge, discipline,* and *intentionality.***

What Is Money?

"My life revolves around money!" I always begin with that phrase when speaking in an auditorium filled with kids, trying to catch their attention. One of the great jobs my wife and I have found in our careers is talking to kids of all ages about money. We love helping young minds understand the role money plays in their lives, and it's always fun to see their eyes light up when we connect the dots for them. Kids are smart.

We begin by sharing a bit about ourselves, explaining, "We own a financial firm and work as financial advisors, helping people make smart money decisions. Over the years, we've personally managed, helped with, consulted on, and grown billions of dollars for people all around the world." I usually tell them with a smile, "You could probably say that our lives revolve around money! But guess what? So does yours. Everything has a cost: your house and car, food, travel, and entertainment… every second of every day costs."

A crucial first step to becoming Rich by Choice is understanding money. So, what *is* money? We encounter money daily, passed from hand to hand, stored in wallets, and transferred between accounts. But when you break it down, money is nothing more than a piece of paper. Yet, for something so small and seemingly simple, it carries immense power in our lives.

On its own, money is neutral, unbiased, and abnormal—neither good nor bad. It's a tool, like a hammer, that can be used to build something beautiful or, if mishandled, can cause damage. Warren Buffett said, "The more you learn, the more you earn." But he really meant that wealth isn't just about accumulating money; it's about understanding how to use it.

It's Not Your Fault

Right now, if you are stressed about money and finances, it's going to be okay. Please understand… *It's not your fault.* Really. It's no wonder so many Americans experience financial stress. Money management is something most of us have never been taught. From childhood, we learn reading, writing, and arithmetic, but how often did anyone sit down and show us how to manage one of life's most important tools? This lack of financial education has left many overwhelmed by their finances, but here's the truth: It's not your fault. We've been expected to navigate the complexities of money without the training to do so. The good news is that no matter where you are in life, it's never too late to change that.

Parents often assume children will learn about money from school. Did you know that 90 percent of kids learn everything about money from their parents? That sounds promising until you realize that 87 percent of parents think their children are learning about money at school.[39] This disconnect creates a confusing mess. This paradox reveals a major problem: no one fully teaches financial literacy. We were never equipped or empowered, and we are all left to navigate this crucial life skill on our own.

Empowering Your Financial Foundation

Without a proper financial foundation, many people feel trapped by their circumstances. In fact, a recent study found that a staggering 2 out of 3 Americans can't pass a basic financial literacy test.[40] But this doesn't have to be your story. Albert Einstein said, "Education is not the learning of facts, but the training of the mind to think."

The good news is that it's never too late to start. Once you start to understand how money works, you gain power over it rather than letting it control you. You have the ability to create lasting change and build the financial peace you deserve. Start today by visiting MichelsFamilyCorporation. com or scanning the QR below to access the Life-Stage Money Education. This is a series of educational videos and content categorized by the current Life-Stage you are in and what money education could benefit you the most.

• • •

It's undeniable. Money impacts every aspect of our lives. It is everywhere, affects everyone, influences everything, and *confuses most*. Everything we do comes with a cost. Every moment, every decision, from the simplest daily choices to the big, life-altering ones, carries a financial impact. Understanding how to manage money effectively can be the key difference between a life filled with financial stress and uncertainty or an empowered one built on security and freedom.

Control, especially financial control, relieves stress and worry. With clearly defined goals, strategies, plans, tactics, and actions, your finances will be stronger, you will have a plan working for you, and you will have control.

To explore resources from this book, scan the QR code or visit RichByChoiceBook.com/bonus.

Nick and Chelsea's Empowering Thoughts

The scent of freshly cut grass and the distant hum of a well-struck driver filled the air as I wiped down another dust-covered golf cart. The Texas sun painted my arms in golden streaks of sweat. It was my daily grind—cleaning carts, gathering scattered range balls, and hauling trash. But Rex, the golf course owner, saw something in me beyond the routine of my minimum-wage job. With a knowing smile and a twinkle in his eye, he'd pull up a chair at the clubhouse and say, "You ready to play?" The game wasn't golf; it was "Who Wants to Be a Millionaire?"—a mental showdown where the prize wasn't imaginary wealth but the key to something far greater: financial freedom. With every question, every lesson, he unlocked a new way of thinking. He didn't just teach me about money; he handed me the blueprint to build a future far beyond the fairways of that small-town course.

Under the fluorescent glow of the pro shop, with my dirt-stained paycheck in hand, Rex ran the numbers. "Just a little," he'd say, "put a little away each month, let time do its magic, and watch what happens." He scribbled figures on a napkin, compound interest stacking like neatly placed poker chips, and for the first time in my life, I saw it—the possibility. The weight of my past, the struggles, and the limitations I once believed were permanent all felt lighter. I wasn't just a kid scrubbing carts anymore. I was an investor. A future millionaire in the making. That feeling—that electric surge of empowerment—never left me. It was the day I realized I wasn't bound by circumstance. My future was mine to create. And that? That was worth more than any paycheck.

3

Happiness by Choice
True Joy Begins with Clarity,
Not Currency.

John and Sarah had always dreamed of their golden years filled with travel, laughter, and a peaceful home to welcome their grandchildren. But for years, their dream seemed distant. Every night, as they sat together at the kitchen table, their conversations were clouded with worries about their finances. Retirement was approaching fast, and though they had worked hard their entire lives, they felt unsure and unprepared. Their savings didn't seem enough, and every unexpected expense felt like a weight that pulled them further from the life they longed for.

Then, one day, everything changed. A close friend introduced them to a new financial advisor, someone who didn't just talk about numbers but about life. He listened to their fears and hopes, and John and Sarah felt truly seen for the first time. Their advisor walked them through the fundamentals—simple yet powerful principles they had never fully embraced. He showed them how to balance giving, saving, spending, investing, budgeting, and earning in a way that aligned with their values.

They began by budgeting with intention, prioritizing what truly mattered to them, whether it was spending time with family or supporting causes close to their hearts. They learned the importance of giving, not just for tax benefits but for the joy and fulfillment it brought into their lives. Saving became a habit they embraced with pride, watching their emergency fund grow and provide the peace of mind they had longed for. And then, there was the magic of investing.

Now, John and Sarah sit on their porch in the evening, sipping tea and reflecting on the journey that brought them to this point. Their lives are filled with joy, not because they have mountains of money, but because they have freedom—from financial worry, to give generously, and to spend time doing what they love.

They found true happiness not through luck but through thoughtful planning and the guidance of someone who showed them how to turn their worries into wealth. In the end, they realized that their happiness wasn't just in the money they had but in the life they had built with it.

The Ultimate Goal: Happiness

John Lennon once said, "When I was five years old, my mother always told me that happiness was the key to life. When I went to school, they asked me what I wanted to be when I grew up. I wrote down 'happy.' They told me that I didn't understand the assignment, and I told them that they didn't understand life."

As you read the statistics in Chapter 2, what thoughts crossed your mind? *Ninety percent of Americans are stressed about money. Seventy percent are experiencing extreme stress.*

Do you see yourself in any of those numbers? Are you stressed or worried? When you think about your financial life, are you truly confident with where you stand? Are you living the life you've always envisioned? As you imagine your future, are you on the right path?

If there's a feeling tugging at you, listen to it. That quiet voice or unease you're feeling comes from your innermost self—the place where you can't hide behind justifications or excuses. It's where the real truth resides. You can't escape the person staring back at you in the mirror. In that space, deep within, are you truly happy? Are you free from worry and fear? If your answer is "no," that's perfectly okay. Keep reading.

In a word, answer these questions:

- What is the most important thing you want in life?
- What do you want for your kids and grandkids?

The answer to all of these questions: happiness! We all strive for happiness for ourselves and those we care about most. Whether we're thinking about our careers, relationships, or the futures of our children, the specifics—whether they become doctors, artists, or real estate agents—are secondary to one core desire: that they find true happiness. At the heart of every parent's dream is not the title or status but the hope that their children will lead joyful, fulfilling lives.

Steve Jobs once said:

I reached the pinnacle of success in the business world. In others' eyes, my life is an epitome of success. However, aside from work, I have little joy. Wealth, in fact, is only a life experience I have gained. At this moment, lying on the sick bed and recalling my whole life, I realize that all recognition and wealth that I took so much pride in have paled and become meaningless in the face of impending death.

His message is clear: Money, by itself, won't bring lasting happiness. The secret is using money purposefully to support what matters most. When managed well, it becomes a tool for peace, joy, and adventure. When misused, it invites stress and hardship.

Happiness is life's ultimate goal. Aristotle called it the purpose of life, and philosophers like Socrates defined it as the enjoyment of what is good and beautiful. Yet, too often, we chase happiness without asking: What truly brings me joy?

Happiness is life's ultimate goal.

Lasting happiness is deeply personal and subjective.[41] What fulfills you won't be the same for someone else, and that's okay. The key is to define your own happiness—know what you're seeking and why. Only then can you create a life aligned with purpose, joy, and peace.

The journey to happiness begins with self-awareness. Once you know what makes your heart sing, you can take steps toward creating a life that aligns with your vision of happiness.

Financial Happiness

Being Rich by Choice starts with understanding what true wealth is to you. True wealth encompasses peace, freedom, joy, memorable experiences, loving relationships, exciting adventures, fulfillment, and living the life you most desire. At its very core, this is Financial Happiness. It goes beyond mere monetary success. It's about cultivating a positive and mindful relationship with our finances, steering our financial journey with intention and joy, because it is not money you want but what money can do for you. It is not a distant dream; it's a living, breathing reality we can all embrace together.

Financial Happiness also encompasses:

- Empowering yourself to use money as a tool to live the life you want.
- Striking a balance between spending, saving, investing, budgeting, and giving.
- Taking control of your financial situation and your future.
- Learning to use money to enhance and protect what is most important to you.
- Leading a life rich in purpose, fulfillment, and well-being.
- Having the freedom to create lifelong memories with loved ones.
- Enabling you to teach your loved ones about money and finance while significantly elevating your family's future.

Happiness is not something ready-made.
It comes from your own actions.

—Dalai Lama

What if you could design your life around what truly makes you happy? Not just the fleeting kind of happiness that comes from a temporary high, but deep, soul-filling, wake-up-every-morning-excited happiness. Too often, we chase money, thinking it will bring fulfillment, only to find that financial success without purpose feels empty. Real wealth isn't just measured in dollars; it's measured in joy, in freedom, in waking up each day excited about the life you've built.

So far, this book has taken you on a journey of understanding, empowerment, and choice. In Chapter 1, you saw how challenges and hardships don't define your future; they shape your resilience. You read about struggles but also about the power of taking control, of refusing to be a victim, and of making the choice to rise. In Chapter 2, we explored the harsh reality that money is the number one cause of stress in most people's lives. Sadly, 90% of Americans feel financial stress, and 72% experience it at extreme levels. But here's the truth: It doesn't have to be this way. You have the power to change your financial story, to move from stress to peace, from uncertainty to confidence. And that journey begins not with numbers but with clarity—understanding what truly brings you happiness.

> **Real wealth isn't just measured in dollars; it's measured in joy, in freedom, in waking up each day excited about the life you've built.**

Before we dive into financial strategies, it's time for a moment of reflection, because money is just a tool, and without knowing what truly brings you happiness, no amount of wealth will ever be enough. This exercise is simple but powerful. Look back over your life and remember the moments when you felt the most alive. Was it a lazy Saturday morning with your kids or grandkids? A long road trip with your best friends? The pride of accomplishing something you once thought was impossible? Those moments hold the key to your financial future because they reveal what truly matters to you. Your challenge now is to use money as a tool to create more of those moments.

This is your first step to financial happiness—mapping out what brings you joy and designing your financial future around it. Because the goal isn't just to be rich; it's to be rich in happiness, rich in purpose, and rich in a life you love. Let's begin.

The Happiness Reflection Exercise (Mapping Your Joy)

Research from positive psychology suggests that reflecting on past joy increases well-being and life satisfaction.[42] This exercise will help you identify the moments in your life when you were happiest so you can align your financial decisions with what truly fulfills you.

Instructions

1. **Look back on your life and identify 3 moments when you felt truly happy.**

   - What were you doing?
   - Who were you with?
   - What made that moment so special?

- Why did this bring you so much joy and
peace?

2. **Write down the key themes that emerge from these moments.**

- Did they involve adventure, relationships, creativity, giving, or something else?
- What values or passions do these moments reflect?

3. **Now, connect it to your financial future.**

- How can you use money as a tool to create more of these experiences?
- What financial goals align with these sources of joy?

Proven Research Data

Studies in positive psychology show that reflecting on peak experiences enhances emotional resilience, reduces stress, and promotes a long-term sense of well-being.[43]

Specific Benefits

- Increases clarity on what truly brings you happiness.
- Helps align financial goals with personal fulfillment.
- Reinforces gratitude and positive emotions.

Examples from Nick

Here are some inspiring examples from families I've had the privilege of working with. Each story is a glimpse into moments of true happiness. As you read, let these experiences spark your own memories. Reflect on the times when you felt most alive and most fulfilled—what were you doing, and who were you with? These moments hold powerful clues to what brings you joy and meaning in life.

The Day I Helped Someone in Need: The Power of Generosity and Meaning

I'll never forget the look on her face. A young mother at the grocery store, fumbling through her purse, her face turning red with embarrassment as she realized she didn't have enough to pay for her groceries. Without thinking, I handed the cashier my card and said, "I've got this." She looked at me, eyes filled with gratitude, and whispered, "Thank you. You have no idea what this means." At that moment, I realized that true wealth isn't about what you have; it's about what you can give.

Key Themes: Generosity, kindness, impact, fulfillment

Financial Connection: I want to build wealth not just for myself but so I can give freely. I will create a budget that prioritizes giving and invest in causes that align with my values.

Grandchildren Laughing in the Backyard: The Power of Presence and Joy

The sprinkler sprayed arcs of water across the backyard as my grandkids shrieked with laughter, jumping in and out, their little feet leaving wet footprints on the grass. I stood there, watching them, feeling the warm summer sun on my face, a cold drink in my hand, and a deep, quiet contentment settled in my chest. This was it. It wasn't the expensive vacations or the fancy toys; it was the small, everyday moments of joy that made life beautiful.

Key Themes: Family, exciting memories, presence, gratitude, simple pleasures

Financial Connection: I want to prioritize time with my family over material possessions. I will make financial decisions that allow me to have more of these moments—whether that means working fewer hours, saving for experiences instead of things, or investing in a home that fosters these memories.

A Cabin in the Mountains: The Power of Simplicity and Connection

The smell of pine filled the crisp morning air as I sipped hot cocoa on the wooden deck of a small cabin, the sun rising over the mountains. My family was still inside, bundled in blankets, laughter spilling from the kitchen as my dad made his famous pancakes. There were no deadlines, no phones buzzing, just the sound of birds, the crackling fire, and the feeling of complete presence. It wasn't luxury that made me happy, but simplicity—being surrounded by those I love in a place that felt like home.

Key Themes: Connection, fun travel, simplicity, freedom, nature, slowing down

Financial Connection: I want to create more moments like this. Maybe it means budgeting for family trips, saving for a vacation home, or structuring my work in a way that gives me more time to be present with those I love.

The Day We Paid Off Our Debt: The Power of Freedom and Security

I'll never forget the day we made the final payment. My spouse and I sat at the kitchen table, staring at the computer screen as we typed in the last payment on our mountain of debt. *Click. Paid. Done.* We looked at each other in silence and then... pure, unfiltered joy. Tears welled up in our eyes as we hugged, knowing that from that moment on, we were free. No more sleepless nights, no more anxiety every time the phone rang. We had taken back control.

Key Themes: Freedom, security, empowerment, resilience

Financial Connection: Moving forward, I want to stay financially free. I will save for the future, invest wisely, and spend with intention so that I never feel that kind of financial stress again.

Creating the Life You Want

"Would you tell me, please, which way I ought to go from here?"
"That depends a good deal on where you want to get to,"
said the Cat.
—Lewis Carroll, *Alice's Adventures in Wonderland*

Begin with the end in mind.

—Stephen R. Covey, *The 7 Habits of Highly Effective People*

Before you move forward, take a few seconds to reflect, because you are about to embark on a life-changing journey that will transform your future in ways you never imagined. But here's the truth: If you don't know where you're going, you are probably going to end up somewhere you do not want to be, with a life you do not want. Clarity is power, and the life you dream of won't happen by accident; it happens by design. So pause, take a little time, and think about what has truly brought you joy because the path to financial happiness starts with knowing exactly where you want to go.

By viewing money as a tool for creating a fulfilling life rather than a source of stress, we open ourselves up to a wonderful world of possibilities. This involves setting goals that align with your values, being kind to yourself during financial challenges, and celebrating every small victory along the way with loved ones.

What defines a fulfilling and happy life is unique for each of us. It's not better or worse than someone else's—it's simply different. And that's beautiful. The ultimate goal is not to compare but to know, deep down, what will make *you* happy and design your life around that vision. As you're reading these words, I know you already have a sense of what that life looks like. You know your dreams, your desires, and your goals.

Money is always secondary to happiness. It has no real value unless used to enhance, protect, and bring joy to yourself and those you cherish most. True wealth is found in the moments, relationships, and dreams that fill your heart, not in a bank account balance. Most important is taking the time to deeply understand what will truly make you happy, what fuels your soul. Once you've discovered that, you can begin using money as the tool it was meant to be and turn those dreams into reality, creating a life filled with purpose, love, and fulfillment.

To explore resources from this book, scan the QR code or visit RichByChoiceBook.com/bonus.

Nick and Chelsea's Happiness:
The Joy of Experiencing Life Together

Imagine the laughter and joy of family adventures, whether it's exploring the hidden corners of our world or just revealing the beautiful simplicities of life together. Being Rich by Choice and Financial Happiness means the freedom to experience these moments without the looming worry of cost.

I love creating exciting experiences with loved ones. It's about saying "yes" to impromptu trips, educational opportunities, and new things that enrich our souls and broaden our horizons.

- The time my son's face lit up the first time he jumped off a waterfall in Hawaii.

- Seeing my daughter filled with excitement when she beat me in a go-kart race for the first time.

- Every morning at Family Camp when Brooks was 3, he would sprint 150 yards like a "man on a mission" to be the first one at breakfast.

- When I was coaching and saw my daughter's face light up with excitement when she scored her first goal.

- The privilege of watching my kids grow as we all take guitar lessons together.

- Seeing my wife jump with thrill as we all sprang from our hiding places to ambush her with Nerf darts as she walked into the house.

- Crying tears of joy after baptizing my daughter.

- Dance and cooking lessons with my wife.

- Quietly watching my children play and laugh together, enjoying the wonderful bliss of childhood.

- Hearing my son laughing at me after he shot me in the "behind" during a father vs son's paintball match at church camp.

- Watching my amazing wife being an incredible mother to our greatest assets. (This is one of my favorite joys in life.)

These shared moments are the ones that bond us tighter. They become the loving memories that will comfort us in times of hardship and dance through our minds during moments of joy. Creating lasting experiences together will be memories we will all have forever.

4

Emotion by Choice
It's Not Money You Want;
It's What Money Can Do for You.

Without fail, when I speak at financial events, I always start with the same line: "I'm here to help you become rich and wealthy. Is that okay with you?" The crowd responds in a chorus of enthusiasm, "YES!" Then I ask, "When do you want to retire?" The answer, nearly unanimous, is always "TODAY!" and "RIGHT NOW!" with every hand raised. I smile and say, "Wonderful." And then, I pose the third question: "Specifically, how much money do you need to live the life you want?" That's when everything changes. The room falls silent. The buzz of excitement evaporates, replaced by a profound stillness. Not a single word is spoken, and you could hear a pin drop.

Why does this question stop people in their tracks? Because most people, while eager for wealth, have never truly considered what it would take to live the life of their dreams. The concept of Financial Freedom, of *living* richly and becoming Rich by Choice, isn't tied to a dollar amount; it's tied to something deeper. This journey we're on together isn't just about acquiring wealth; it's about the fulfillment that money can help bring to your life: Money Emotions.

Success without fulfillment is the ultimate failure.

—Tony Robbins

Cynithia's Money Emotion

When I first met Cynthia 15 years ago, she was a woman shattered by the weight of her circumstances. Struggling through a devastating divorce, her entire world was crumbling, and the pain she carried was written all over her face. As she sat across from me in that first meeting, she couldn't hold back the tears. They flowed uncontrollably like a river rushing through the Montana mountains as the snow began to melt—wild, unstoppable, and heart-wrenching. She was lost, hurt, and afraid, trapped in the anguish of leaving a marriage that had been nothing short of a nightmare.

Cynthia poured out her heart, sharing the details of her broken marriage, each word laced with heartache and sorrow. It was as though the weight of her pain filled the room, and I found myself at a loss for words. I knew nothing I could say would make her feel better at that moment. Sometimes, people don't need advice—they just need someone to listen, be present, and care. So, I sat there quietly, my heart aching for her, offering her the only thing I could at that time: compassion and understanding.

As the weeks turned into months and the divorce process slowly came to a close, Cynthia's tears began to fade, replaced by a quiet strength that I hadn't seen in those early meetings. She was resilient, intelligent, and determined. Despite the emotional wreckage she had endured, Cynthia was motivated to build a new life—a life where she would never again be at the mercy of someone else's choices.

One day, as we worked through the same financial exercises you're learning, Cynthia's Money Emotion came into sharp focus. "Independence," she said, her voice steady yet filled with resolve. I remember it so clearly, the moment her eyes, though still sad, held a spark of determination. "I never want to have to depend on anyone ever again," she whispered, her voice a little stronger now. "I want to be financially independent for the rest of my life."

That moment changed everything. I watched as Cynthia transformed from a woman who felt broken by her circumstances into someone who was rebuilding her life from the ground up—on her own terms. It was inspiring to witness her reclaim her power, not just financially but emotionally as well.

Cynthia's story is a testament to the strength we all have within us, even when life feels unbearably difficult. She showed me—and herself—that no matter how dark things seem, there is always hope, always a way forward. All it takes is the courage to believe in yourself and the determination to never give up. Cynthia's life instantly started to improve the very moment she discovered her Money Emotion.

What Money Represents: Freedom, Joy, and Peace

It's not the money you want; it's what money can do for you. You might be reading this and thinking, *"Wait, Nick, I do want more money! More money is exactly what I need to be happy."* And I understand. But let me explain.

When I first meet with clients like Jim and Lisa from Chapter 2, they often dive straight into the numbers: how much they've saved, what they've invested, and what they're earning. While that information is important, I always pause and say, "We'll

> **It's not the money you want; it's what money can do for you.**

get to that. But first, let's talk about what really matters: you and your family." I care more about the people behind the money than the money itself. Why? Because money is simply a tool, and if you don't know what you truly want, that tool is useless.

Before we can make any progress, you have to understand your Money Emotions. What does money mean to you? What emotions does it stir up? What lifestyle are you striving for, and what would truly make you feel fulfilled? These questions are the foundation of your journey to Financial Happiness.

What it comes down to is it's not money you want; it's the emotions, the experiences, and the lifestyle that money allows. Using money intentionally can create positive emotions: freedom, joy, security, and peace.

The Power of Money as a Tool

I want to teach you how to use money as a tool to shape your best life. Understanding the role of money and how to wield it effectively can help you fulfill your dreams, build a secure future, and enjoy the life you've always envisioned. It's not just about making money; it's about making money *work* for you, aligning with your values and dreams.

As you read this, you probably have some idea of the emotions and experiences you want, but let's take it deeper. *What do you truly want from life, and why?* Everyone's answer is different, and that's the beauty of it. Your vision is unique, and so is your path to get there.

Over the years, I've learned that while we may all speak the same language, we often interpret words very differently. This is especially true when it comes to money and the emotions associated with it. J.K. Rowling once said, "Words are our most inexhaustible source of magic." They have the power to shape our thoughts, stir our emotions, and inspire us. Depending on how we interpret them, they can create joy or cause pain.

What would you say if I asked you about your Money Emotions?

I want more money because I want more _____.

Maybe you'd say freedom, fun, security, peace, or something else entirely. Whatever your answer is, that's wonderful, but I urge you to take it a step further. *What does that word truly mean to you? Why do you want more of it? What does that life look like?* It's important to remember that this is all subjective—what freedom means to one person may be completely different for another, and that's okay. Your desires aren't better or worse than anyone else's, just unique to you.

Earlier, I asked you to think about your Money Emotions. Money Emotions are simply the feelings money brings into your life. Ultimately, it's not the money itself that you're after. What you truly desire are the emotions that money can help you achieve.

So, let's dig into what you really want. Your desired Money Emotions are:

- **Peace**—a deep sense of calm, knowing that everything is taken care of
- **Freedom**—the ability to live your life on your terms
- **Flexibility**—having the choice to do what you want when you want
- **Security**—the comfort of knowing your future and your family's future are protected
- **Happiness**—the joy that comes from living a life aligned with your values
- **Joy**—a deep sense of contentment
- **Power**—the strength to take control of your destiny
- **The ability to help others**—the fulfillment that comes from giving back.
- **More time with loved ones**—precious moments shared without financial stress
- **Fulfillment**—the deep satisfaction that comes from living with purpose
- **Independence**—freedom from relying on anyone else for your financial well-being
- **A sense of accomplishment**—knowing you've achieved something meaningful
- **A sense of meaning**—the understanding that your life has purpose
- **A worry-free life**—the peace that comes from letting go of financial anxiety
- **A stress-free life**—the release of financial tension and strain

- **To find your purpose**—a life where your work and passions align
- **To be the best version of yourself**—the journey of self-improvement and growth
- **To live your best life**—whatever that means to you, filled with passion and excitement
- **To have more fun**—to enjoy life's moments without worrying about finances
- **To have more adventures**—to explore the world and create memories
- **To gain confidence**—to believe in yourself and your financial choices
- **To meet new people**—to expand your social circle and experiences
- **To create new memories**—to make lasting moments with those who matter
- **To be loved, admired, and respected**—to feel valued by others
- **To prove to yourself and others that you could do it**—to achieve your goals and feel proud
- **To belong**—to feel a part of something bigger than yourself

Take a moment to reflect on which of these emotions resonates most with you. These are the real reasons we strive for more money. Circle all that apply to you. It's not about the numbers in your bank account; it's about the life you want to create. It's about unlocking the emotions that allow you to thrive, grow, and feel fulfilled.

Why do you want more money? What Money Emotion are you truly seeking? Once you identify that, you can begin to align your financial goals with your emotional desires—and that's when real transformation begins.

Rich by Choice Formula

Right here, at this intersection of dreams and strategy, is where my passion truly comes to life. What I love most about my work is learning what will make someone truly happy and then using the best strategies to help them achieve it. There's something incredibly powerful about connecting someone's deepest desires with a clear, actionable plan. This is where Financial Happiness is born—when your emotions and goals align with a strategy that brings those dreams to life.

Too often, we make broad, well-intentioned statements like, "I want to save more" or "I want to retire." While these are admirable, they don't provide the clarity needed to actually change your life—they're too vague to drive real results.

Now, it's your turn. Here's where it gets personal. I want you to ask yourself:

- *What emotions are you really seeking and why?*
- *What is it you want from your money, and why?*

The answer to this question is where everything starts. Cynthia wanted financial independence so she would never have to rely on someone ever again. She never wanted to feel pain and hardship again. Who could blame her? Once you've determined the life you want and, more importantly, *why* you want that life, everything begins to fall into place.

Here's the formula to bridge the gap between your desires and the life you envision:

> **Desired emotion** → **What will bring that emotion** → **SMART goal**
>
> (SMART goals are Specific, Measurable, Attainable, Relevant, Time-framed.)

Let me give you some real-world examples:

- **I want peace.** → I want to experience financial peace so I can sleep at night without worrying about bills piling up. Financial peace will allow me to focus on enjoying life and stop feeling the constant pressure of debt and financial uncertainty.

- **I want freedom.** → I want the freedom to never work again for my rude boss who belittles me. Financial freedom will allow me to spend more time with my family and friends and pursue my passion projects without the constant stress of needing to earn a paycheck.

- **I want security and confidence.** → I want to feel secure knowing that my family and lifestyle are protected. Security gives me the confidence to enjoy life without fear of unexpected financial hardships, knowing that everything is taken care of.

- **I want purpose and passion.** → I want to live a life of purpose by giving back to my community. Contributing to the next generation will give me a sense of fulfillment that money alone can't provide.

- **I want adventure and excitement.** → I want to travel the world, experiencing new cultures and adventures without the fear of running out of money in retirement. Financial security in retirement will allow me to create lifelong memories with my family, free of worry.

Now, it's your turn to take control of your future. What Money Emotion are you seeking, and what will bring it to your life? This is the moment to be specific, get crystal clear about what you want, and create a SMART goal that will make it a reality. Use this framework to guide your journey.

→ **I want** (desired emotion):

_____

→ **What will bring that emotion**:

_____

→ **SMART goal** (specific, measurable, attainable, relevant, and time-framed):

_____

If you cannot come up with a SMART goal at this moment, that is okay. You will be able to by the time you finish this book. To complete this exercise, simply put what you are willing to do/sacrifice to accomplish your desired emotion.

- **(Example with SMART GOAL) I want free-dom** → I want the freedom to never work again for my rude boss who belittles me. Financial freedom will allow me to spend more time with my family and friends and pursue my passion projects without the constant stress of needing to earn a paycheck → Save 10 percent of my paycheck into a diversified investment portfolio, reaching an exact dollar amount that will safely generate a lifelong income by a specific date (SMART goal).

- **(EXAMPLE without SMART GOAL, but with personal sacrifices) I want freedom** → I want the freedom to never work again for my rude boss who belittles me. Financial freedom will allow me to spend more time with my family and friends and pursue my passion projects without the constant stress of needing to earn a paycheck.

  They might give up dining out frequently, shopping for the latest trends, or taking extravagant vacations. Instead, they'd focus on budgeting and redirecting those funds into savings, investments, or debt repayment.

This exercise isn't just about money—it's about using money as a tool to create the life you truly want. So don't settle for vague hopes and dreams. Dive deeper, define what will bring you happiness, and map out the steps to get there. Your future self will thank you for it.

The joy of my work is helping people uncover their true desires and then implementing the best financial strategies to bring them to life. Once you know the life you want and *why* you want it, we can build a customized roadmap to get you there. This is about more than just saving money or retiring—it's about building a life that brings you fulfillment, joy, and Financial Happiness.

• • •

Now it's your turn to reflect and take action. What emotions are you seeking? What lifestyle will bring you the most joy? And what steps can you take today to begin creating that life? (Remember, it's not money you want; it's what money can do for you. It's the life that money can help you create.)

To explore resources from this book, scan the QR code or visit RichByChoiceBook.com/bonus.

Nick and Chelsea's Financial Emotions

Fear is a reaction. Courage is a decision.

—Winston Churchill

When Chelsea and I were newly married, the weight of the unknown felt like a heavy fog settling over my chest. I was excited, yes, but beneath that excitement was a quiet, gnawing fear. *Could I provide for us? Would we have enough? What about the responsibilities we couldn't even see coming yet?* The future felt overwhelming, a distant storm I wasn't sure I was prepared to face.

I found myself so caught up in the here and now—paying bills, making ends meet, figuring out this new life together—that I lost sight of what was ahead. Without a clear vision, I wasn't motivated to save, invest, or even think about building something greater. I was drifting, reacting instead of creating. But everything changed when Chelsea and I sat down, heart to heart, and put pen to paper, defining not just what we wanted today but the life we wanted to build for tomorrow. That single act of clarity lit a fire in us, transforming hesitation into confidence and fear into fuel.

Together, Chelsea and I created our vision statement for our lives (short, intermediate, and long-term goals), essentially everything we wanted to accomplish in our lives.

We noticed that our passion for saving and investing suddenly increased because we had a purpose. We were encouraged and inspired. Together, we created:

- Freedom
- Peace for our future

- Security for our family
- Exciting, life-long memories together
- A legacy for our children

Have you taken the time to examine your financial emotions and create a vision statement for your future?

5

Relationships by Choice Your "Why" Deserves a Powerful "Who."

Years into my marriage, my life had officially come full circle, and the memories I buried deep inside rose to the surface again. The very issue I dedicate my life to solving for others—financial stress—had crept back into my own life. This brought with it the same pain and tension I knew as a child, this time affecting my marriage. The weight of financial strain was starting to take its toll on us, and I again found myself at a crossroads. I had two choices: Do nothing and let the tension grow, or search for answers. For me, the choice is clear. My family is my reason why—why I strive, why I endure, and why I refuse to settle. So, I set out on a journey to find the answers, determined to make things better for the people I love the most.

It might sound unusual, especially coming from a financial planner, but my journey to genuine wealth and happiness didn't begin with a breakthrough in business or a financial windfall. It started with my marriage. For most of my life, I believed that "wealth" was synonymous with money. But as life unfolded, I realized that true wealth encompasses much more. It's about relationships, fulfillment, growth, purpose, and harmony in all areas of life.

The Power of Partnership: A Journey to True Wealth

Most people, myself included, assume that financial security guarantees happiness in marriage. But that isn't the case. You see it in the media: Famous people with millions of dollars still find themselves divorced, broken, and unhappy. That stark reality highlights the truth: money alone can't bring happiness. Something deeper is required. The statistics shared in Chapter 2 showed that when finances are misaligned or unaddressed in a marriage, they create tension that can quietly corrode even the strongest of relationships. I had to learn this firsthand.

When Chelsea and I got married, I assumed, as many financial professionals do, that because of my expertise, I should handle all of our finances. It seemed logical. I was the advisor; it was my realm. But in hindsight, I was wrong. I was young and dumb. I managed everything alone, and Chelsea, understandably, didn't have a clear picture of our financial life. She trusted that everything was going well because the investments were paying off. But without transparency or shared decision-making, we slipped into a dangerous pattern. Like many couples, we began spending more and more, confident that our income and investments would sustain it all. It wasn't long before we made some money mistakes, and the weight of those choices began to push us backward. As you might guess, those financial missteps led to arguments.

Now, if I'm being honest, our marriage wasn't in trouble. We were like most couples, arguing from time to time, but nothing too alarming. Still, deep down, I felt unsettled. Life was supposed to be better. I was a successful businessman, working hard and doing what I loved. We had money in the bank, a great family, and a comfortable life. On paper, everything looked perfect. Yet, something was missing, and I couldn't quite put my finger on it.

Despite the appearance of success, our financial life and, by extension, our marriage weren't what I had envisioned. I saw my future looking very similar to my past. It scared me. I knew something had to change. I needed answers—answers that would not only help our finances but would transform our marriage. My "why" became crystal clear: my family. I wanted more than just good; I wanted great. And so, I began searching for the missing piece.

As I dug deeper, two transformative things happened, and I believe both were divinely inspired. The first was reading a few recommended books by my mentor, not on finance, but on women and relationships. This book opened my eyes to a simple yet profound truth: When Chelsea and I got married, we became one. In every aspect of our lives, including finances, we needed to act as one. I hadn't been honoring that. I had unintentionally left her out of one of the most crucial areas of our lives. This needed to change.

Life was moving at full speed—marriage, family, kids, career. Maybe you can relate. The days filled up, responsibilities piled on, and before we knew it, the things that mattered most started slipping into the background.

Somewhere along the way, I realized something important: I had never truly paused to ask Chelsea what she wanted. What were her dreams? Her thoughts? How did she envision our life together, not just as a family, but as partners in every aspect, including our finances?

I had been so focused on providing and pushing forward that I hadn't taken the time to truly listen. To understand. To build something together, not just for us but with us. That realization changed everything.

What about you? When was the last time you stopped the whirlwind of life to ask the people you love what truly matters to them?

Maybe you were raised in a home where the man handled all the money, or perhaps it was your mother who took charge of the finances. Regardless of the roles you witnessed growing up, I'm here to tell you that creating a financial plan together is essential. Your marriage is a partnership, and together, you move forward toward a better future. When both voices are heard, respected, and valued, it creates a foundation for not only financial success but a stronger marriage.

When I began to see Chelsea's role in our finances as equally important as my own, everything changed. Her happiness became evident, and I realized just how much I had been missing out on by not including her earlier. Since then, Chelsea and I have made

Creating a financial plan together is essential.

every financial decision together: the budget, investments, future planning, business decisions—all of it. We even hold "Michels Family Financial Meetings," and I've come to love those discussions.

Chelsea's insights and intelligence are remarkable. She has been one of the greatest assets to our financial life, a blessing

I had neglected to recognize. Our finances have flourished, and it's clear that once we embraced this concept of unity, we unlocked the opportunities we had been missing all along. We became fully aligned—two hearts, one vision, moving forward together. No longer just individuals navigating life side by side, we became a unified team, deeply invested in the future we were building. Every decision, every step, every dream—we were in it together, not just as partners but as co-creators of something greater than ourselves. We weren't just involved; we were fully committed, with everything on the line. Our future wasn't just mine or hers—it was *ours*, and we were both all in.

Through my professional experience, I've seen a pattern over and over again: Couples who work together, value each other's opinions, and make decisions as a united front are not only happier but wealthier too—*much wealthier*. In the early and mid-1900s, Andrew Carnegie was the richest man in the world. Napoleon Hill was, and probably still is, the great self-help author in American history. Together, they designed a plan to research and interview over 500 of the most successful people in the world. That research was the basis of the all-time best-selling book *Think and Grow Rich*. In his book, Napoleon Hill describes his Mastermind principle as, "The coordination of knowledge and effort between two or more people who work towards a definite purpose in a spirit of harmony... no two minds ever come together without thereby creating a third, invisible force, which may be likened to a third mind."[44] That harmony between partners can transform everything.

If you haven't included your spouse in your financial decisions, let today be the day you change that. This isn't about simply having them sit at the table while you outline your plans. It's about inviting them into the conversation.

Ask for their opinions. Discuss the "what ifs" together because life is unpredictable, and financial challenges will come. This doesn't mean both of you have to love financial matters equally. It means making decisions as partners, valuing each other's input, and moving forward with a shared vision.

Looking back, I see how something so simple—treating my spouse as a true financial partner—completely transformed my marriage, finances, and life. It was a shift I hadn't realized I needed, but it has been one of the most powerful lessons I've learned. So, my dear friend, I encourage you to honor and value your spouse. Include them in your finances. Watch how it not only improves the dynamic of your marriage but also enhances every area of your life.

> Treating my spouse as a true financial partner completely transformed my marriage, finances, and life.

A Legacy Worth Nurturing

I remember my grandpa's funeral as if it were just yesterday. The soft hum of the old church, the warmth of familiar faces, and the gentle sunlight filtering through the windows filled the room. My heart was heavy, but there was warmth in the air, a sense of love and gratitude filling the space. I sat on the far-right side of the church, the last seat on the outside, about halfway from the front, wearing a charcoal grey suit and a white dress shirt.

My stepdad stood at the podium. His voice was steady yet full of emotion as he spoke about the remarkable man his father was—my grandfather. His words painted a picture of a life lived with purpose and love: a war veteran, a devoted husband and father, a tireless worker, and a man deeply rooted in his faith. I knew these things well, but hearing them spoken aloud was a beautiful tribute to the man we all admired.

Then, my stepdad shared an analogy that stirred something deep within me. He asked us to picture a tranquil pond, surrounded by towering green trees and brimming with life, its waters a perfect crystal blue. He described a rock being tossed into the pond, creating ripples that spread far and wide. My grandpa's life, he said, was that rock, and the positive ripple effect of his love, values, and actions continues to touch us all. At that moment, I realized *I am a part of that ripple*. All the good I strive to do as a father, a husband, a friend, and a man of faith is a reflection of him.

As I carry his legacy forward, I, too, create my own ripple effect. It made me pause and reflect on those who have loved and shaped me and the impact I want to leave behind for those I love. The size, reach, and positive ripple my life creates are within my hands, and it's a legacy worth nurturing. The question he left us with lingers in my heart to this day: Is my life creating the kind of ripple that I want? And how far will my own ripple reach?

Whose ripple effect has positively shaped your life? Whose legacy are you carrying forward? You carry it forward because you are loved. Who do you love? Whose life do you want to have a positive ripple effect on? How big of a positive ripple effect?

Extending Beyond the Family: Sharing Happiness with Others

Becoming Rich by Choice is not just a personal mission; it's a community aspiration. Achieving this stability and joy offers a unique platform to help others. It's about passing on knowledge, lifting others in their times of need, and fostering environments where more people can reach their own heights of financial well-being.

Helping others achieve an amazing life of significance, living their desired life of being Rich by Choice and Financial Happiness, brings me joy and builds a community rooted in support and understanding. It's about creating a ripple effect of positivity and empowerment, reaching far beyond the immediate circle of my family.

Discovering Your Financial Who

I want you to pause for a moment and know this deep in your heart: *You and your loved ones are worth it.* No matter where you are in life, no matter the struggles you've faced or the mistakes you've made, you deserve Financial Happiness. You have the power to create a wonderful ripple effect. You and the people you care about deserve a life filled with peace, joy, and abundance. I'll say it again—*you and your loved ones are worth it.* You are special, and so are they.

I want you to think about your "Financial Who." Who are the people in your life for whom you're doing this? Who are the ones you want to protect, provide for, and inspire? Take a moment to visualize their faces—their smiles, their laughter, their hopes for the future. Write their names down. These are the people who give you purpose, who fill your life with meaning. You've already identified your "Financial Why," but now it's time to focus on your "Who"—the loved ones who drive you to strive for something better.

Why is this important? Because love is the most powerful force in the universe. It gives us strength when we feel weak, courage when we are afraid, and hope when the path ahead seems unclear. Love has a way of igniting a fire inside us, pushing us forward to achieve things we never thought possible. It's the greatest source of inspiration we have.

Think about it: *Who* do you love? Who has sacrificed for you, lifted you up, and supported you through life's challenges? Maybe it's a parent, a spouse, a friend, or your child. Visualize their joy, their dreams, and the life you want to build for them. What do they want for you? What do you want for their future? Let that feeling sink in—your deep love and responsibility for them.

If you're feeling alone right now, know this: *You are still worthy of love.* Even if that love comes from within, that is still your "Who." Loving yourself can be just as transformative as loving others.

Science shows that when we think about the people we love, our brains light up—millions of neurons firing at once, energizing and filling us with purpose. Love can give us the strength to keep going, even when times are tough. It can push us to become the best versions of ourselves and to reach heights we never thought possible. *To love richly is to live richly.*

I don't know your specific challenges, but I do know this: I am deeply grateful for your life because it has brought you to this moment. You're here, reading this because you want something more—for yourself, for your loved ones. If you apply what you learn, your life will transform in ways you can't imagine. It won't happen overnight, but step by step, your life will improve.

Remember: *You and your loved ones are worth it.*

• • •

Every day, driven by the unconditional love for my wife and children, I am committed to this journey of being Rich by Choice. It's a path marked by dreams, laughter, and the promise of a brighter tomorrow. Together, we are not just building wealth; we are crafting a legacy of love, peace, joy, adventure, security, and a life of amazing significance.

To explore resources from this book, scan the QR code or visit RichByChoiceBook.com/bonus.

Nick and Chelsea's Big Who

Becoming Rich by Choice is not just a journey toward prosperity; it's a heartfelt commitment to my wonderful family: my wife and kids. Every step I take on this path is fueled by love, the desire for shared adventures, and the dream of a better future for my loved ones.

Growing up, I experienced my share of challenges, personally witnessing the struggles financial instability can bring and the pain it can cause. Those early years shaped my resolve not to let history repeat itself. As a father and husband, my aspirations go beyond merely providing. I envision a life where financial worries are not a daily concern for my family and where my kids can flourish.

This dream is about crafting a future where my children's talents and passions are nurtured to their fullest potential. It's about replacing the narrative of struggle with one of strength and stability. It's my deepest wish to give them the foundation they need to build incredible lives of their own. Seeing them happy and succeeding in their passions will bring joy to my heart.

Financial Happiness also translates into expressing my love and care in tangible ways. It's about showing my family, through every action and decision, how deeply they are valued. This journey is a testament to my dedication to ensure they feel secure, cherished, and supported at every turn. It brings me joy and fulfillment.

I want my wife and kids to know, without a shadow of a doubt, that they are my priority. Every decision to save, invest, or spend wisely is a declaration of my love, echoing louder than words could.

6

Resilience by Choice
Greatness Lies Just
Beyond the Struggle.

The Colorado Gold Rush, also known as the Pike's Peak Gold Rush, began in 1858 and lasted through the mid-1860s. It was one of the major gold rushes in the United States, drawing thousands of prospectors to the region in search of wealth, and it played a significant role in the settlement and development of Colorado. Almost 103,000 pounds of gold was discovered. That would be worth almost $4,000,000,000 ($4 billion) today. The initial discovery of gold was made near present-day Denver, which led to a surge of settlers heading to the area with the hope of striking it rich.

There's a story in my family inspired by an antidote in Napoleon Hill's *Think and Grow Rich* that perfectly illustrates this, and it has stuck with me throughout my life. It's the story of my great Uncle Buck, a man with dreams as big as the West and a heart full of hope during the mid-1800s when the gold rush was at its peak.

Like many others, Uncle Buck was struck with "gold fever." The allure of striking it rich and the promise of a fortune waiting to be unearthed pulled him to the wild frontier. With a pickaxe in one hand and a shovel in the other, he staked his claim and began the backbreaking work of mining. Day after day, he toiled in the dirt, sweat dripping from his brow, muscles aching, but his determination never wavered. He could almost see the gleam of gold waiting for him just beneath the surface.

After weeks of exhausting labor, his persistence paid off. Uncle Buck hit the first shining piece of ore. It wasn't just any ore; it was rich, promising gold. His heart raced with excitement, and visions of wealth beyond his wildest dreams flooded his mind. Convinced that he had discovered a gold mine, he scraped together the funds to buy the machinery needed to bring the ore to the surface.

The first carload of gold ore was mined and shipped to the smelter, and the results were staggering. The smelter confirmed it was one of the richest mines in the state. My great-uncle was ecstatic. He could already picture the mansion he'd buy, the future filled with luxury. He believed he was on the verge of his fortune.

But then, everything changed. The vein of gold—his dream—disappeared without warning. One day, it was there, and the next, it was gone. He was devastated. Uncle Buck drilled frantically, trying to pick up the lost vein, but it seemed the rainbow had vanished, and the pot of gold was out of reach. His hands, once full of hope, were now empty.

Frustrated and heartbroken, Uncle Buck did what many of us have done in the face of adversity—he quit. He sold his equipment to a poor local man, packed up his shattered dreams, and headed home.

But that's not where the story ends.

The "poor" local man who bought the machinery wasn't ready to give up. He was smart enough to seek help. He called in a mining engineer to take a look. After doing a few calculations, the engineer analyzed the mine carefully and explained that the previous owner had made one critical mistake: He didn't understand the fault lines. According to the engineer, the vein of gold wasn't gone; it was just three feet away from where Uncle Buck had stopped drilling.

Three feet.

Sure enough, the new owner started drilling just three feet beyond where my uncle had given up, and there it was— the rich vein of gold Uncle Buck had been searching for. The "poor" man became super rich, swimming in an ocean of money, all because he sought expert advice and didn't quit too soon.

This story isn't just about gold. It's about how close we can be to achieving our dreams and finding our version of success, but often, we give up just before we strike it. Uncle Buck's story is a reminder that sometimes, the breakthrough we've been working toward is just a little further, just one more step, one more decision, one more call for help away.

Another valuable lesson? Don't be afraid to ask for guidance. Sometimes, all it takes is expert advice to turn a dead end into a gold mine, whether in life, business, or finances. The real tragedy isn't in failing; it's in stopping when you're only three feet from success.

Some of the most successful people in history have

Don't be afraid to ask for guidance.

said that their greatest success came just one step beyond the point at which defeat had overtaken them. So, before you quit, before you walk away, ask yourself, are you just three feet from gold?

The Survivor's Financial Mindset: Finding Purpose to Power Through Challenges

Amidst the suffocating cold and relentless hunger of the Nazi concentration camps, Viktor Frankl walked through a world where death cast its shadow over every breath. Prisoners, reduced to hollow-eyed skeletons, shuffled past barbed wire fences, their existence hanging by a thread of hope or despair. The stench of suffering filled the air, and despair seemed to consume men faster than starvation.

Frankl discovered something extraordinary, a truth so profound that it allowed him to endure horrors most men could not survive. He realized that even when stripped of every possession, dignity, and freedom, a few things remained unbreakable: the freedom to choose one's attitude, the grit to never give up, and the inner power to choose how to respond to life, even in the face of unbearable suffering.

Frankl's discovery was both simple and profound: humans are not defined by what happens to them but by how they respond to what happens to them. In the camps, where death was as common as the sunrise, Frankl saw that those who clung to a greater purpose, whether it was reuniting with loved ones, finishing a life's work, or finding meaning, were the ones who found the strength to survive.

He describes how he endured bitter nights, frozen feet trudging through snow, by imagining his wife's face and speaking to her as if she were right beside him. Even though he didn't know if she was alive, the love he felt kept him going. "He who has a why to live," Frankl quotes Nietzsche, "can bear almost any how."

Viktor Frankl's book, *Man's Search for Meaning*, is more than a memoir of survival; it is a beacon of hope for anyone struggling to find meaning in life's darkest hours.[45] His journey reveals that purpose doesn't eliminate pain but transforms it, making the unbearable bearable and the impossible survivable. The book invites readers to confront their struggles head-on and reminds them that the most powerful human weapon isn't strength or wealth but the ability to find light in the darkest of places and the power to never give up.

But what does this have to do with money? Everything. Financial challenges can feel overwhelming—whether you're drowning in debt, facing unexpected expenses, or trying to stay disciplined during hard economic times. When you're in the thick of it, it's easy to feel trapped, stressed, and hopeless. But like Frankl's story, the path to overcoming financial struggles starts with finding *meaning* in your financial life through a clear *who* and *why*.

Your Financial "Who" and "Why"

- **Your "Who":** Who are you building wealth for? Maybe it's your children, ensuring they never experience the financial hardships you endured. Perhaps it's your partner, creating a future of shared peace and security. Or maybe it's for you—a version of yourself that deserves financial freedom, dignity, and joy. Defining your "who" makes the day-to-day sacrifices meaningful rather than draining.

- **Your "Why"**: What drives your financial journey? Is it retiring early, traveling the world, or living without financial anxiety? Is it creating generational wealth or supporting causes close to your heart? When this purpose is clearly defined, setbacks feel less like permanent defeats and more like temporary challenges on a meaningful path.

Just as Frankl found strength in the midst of unimaginable suffering, you can find strength through financial struggles by holding tight to your financial purpose. If your "who" is your family and your "why" is building a legacy, suddenly, taking action to improve your future is not a sacrifice.

The Power of Controlling Your Reaction

One of Frankl's core teachings was that while we cannot always control what happens to us, we can control our response. In financial terms, you may not be able to prevent every financial crisis—markets crash, jobs are lost, expenses arise—but how you react determines your future.

- **A reaction of panic leads to poor decisions:** impulsive spending, taking on more debt, or abandoning a long-term investment strategy.
- **A reaction grounded in purpose leads to thoughtful action:** creating a plan, cutting unnecessary expenses, seeking advice, and staying the course.

When faced with financial adversity, pause and reflect on your financial "who" and "why." Ask yourself: "How will my actions today affect the future I'm trying to create?" This simple shift in mindset can transform anxiety into resolve.

Attaching Meaning to Financial Setbacks

Frankl believed that meaning could be found even in suffering. The same is true for financial struggles. Losing money in a bad investment, facing unexpected bills, or starting over after financial mistakes isn't the end of the journey—it's part of the story.

Every setback contains a lesson:

- Maybe it's learning the importance of emergency savings after facing a sudden expense.
- Perhaps it's developing the discipline to live within your means after falling into debt.
- Or maybe it's understanding that setbacks aren't failures, just experiments that guide you toward better decisions.

When you attach meaning to financial struggles, they become tools for growth rather than weights dragging you down. Frankl's philosophy reminds us that even when circumstances are out of our control, *our response and mindset are always within our control.*

The Financial Survivor's Mindset

Frankl's ultimate message is one of hope: humans have the power to endure and thrive by finding meaning in the midst of difficulty. For those facing financial hardships, this message is just as powerful. By anchoring yourself to your financial "who" and "why" and controlling your reaction to adversity, you can navigate even the toughest financial challenges and come out stronger.

Your financial freedom is not just about accumulating wealth—it's about creating a life of meaning and purpose. When your money is tied to a clear mission, every dollar saved, invested, or spent brings you closer to the life you're meant to live.

So, when you face your next financial challenge, remember this: the obstacle is not the end. It's the bridge to something greater—if you stay connected to your financial "who" and "why."

Sara Blakely's Inspirational Story: Spanx

Sara Blakely's journey is the story of a woman who turned rejection into a ladder and climbed her way to a billion-dollar empire. In the beginning, her world was filled with closed doors and dead ends. She dreamed of becoming a lawyer, but the LSAT stopped her in her tracks multiple times. Her days were spent selling fax machines door to door under the scorching Florida sun, where she endured endless rejection with each knock that went unanswered or slammed in her face. Yet, even as doubt whispered that she wasn't meant for success, a flicker of creativity refused to die. That flicker became a spark on an ordinary morning as she stood in front of her mirror, cutting the feet off her pantyhose to solve a problem women had silently struggled with for years: comfort, confidence, and the desire for clothes that worked *with* them instead of against them.

Fueled by this moment of ingenuity, Blakely dove into action with relentless determination. She cold-called manufacturers who dismissed her idea as silly or impractical, each rejection threatening to crush her spirit. But she had learned something on those long days of selling fax machines: persistence isn't glamorous, but it's unstoppable. With only $5,000 in savings, Blakely mapped out every detail of her brand while working late nights and sketching her vision on scraps of paper. She knocked on more doors until one finally opened. Her first prototype was born, but the real break-through came when Neiman Marcus agreed to sell her product, changing her life in an instant. What followed was a revolution in women's fashion—a brand built not on cor-porate backing but on grit, resilience, and the unshakable belief that failure is merely a step toward success.

Today, Spanx is a billion-dollar brand, and Blakely is celebrated as a pioneer for female entrepreneurs everywhere. But beyond the financial success lies the heart of her story: She didn't become a billion-aire by chasing perfection; she did it by embracing rejection, learning from failure, and trusting the creative spark within her. Her journey serves

"Failure is not the opposite of success. It's part of the process."

as a reminder that the world often tries to define your limits, but success comes when you defy them. In her framed office sits a note to herself, a simple reminder of the lesson that shaped her life: "Failure is not the opposite of success. It's part of the process."

• • •

These real-life success stories demonstrate that failure isn't the end—it's often the beginning of something incredi-ble. Each person faced rejection, hardship, or loss, but they channeled those experiences into rediscovery and triumph. Their journeys remind us that success is built not on perfection but on persistence, resilience, and the courage to keep going when others stop.

The "Survivor's Mindset" Exercise (Inspired by Viktor Frankl's Teachings)

This exercise is designed to help readers find meaning in their struggles, just as Viktor Frankl did in the concentration camps. By anchoring to their deeper purpose, they can transform setbacks into stepping stones for growth.

Instructions

1. **Define Your "Who" and "Why."**

   o Who are you pushing forward for? (Your family, your future self, your community?)
   o Why does overcoming this challenge matter?

2. **Write down a past hardship you've overcome.**

   o What was the situation?
   o How did you get through it?
   o What strengths did you develop from that experience?

3. **Now, apply those lessons to your current struggles.**

   o What are your three biggest concerns?

o What are their current challenges?

o How can the strength you developed in the past help you today?

o What would your future self tell you about the value of pushing through?

o Identify one small but powerful step you can take today to keep going.

4. **End with a declaration:**

o Write down one sentence declaring your resilience, e.g., *"I have overcome challenges before, and I will overcome this one too."*

Proven Research Data

Viktor Frankl's research in *Man's Search for Meaning* and subsequent psychological studies confirm that individuals who attach meaning to their struggles are significantly more likely to endure hardship and emerge stronger.

Specific Benefits

• Strengthens emotional resilience.

• Reduces stress and anxiety by shifting focus to purpose.

• Reinforces a growth mindset, making setbacks feel more manageable.

Final Thoughts

This exercise helps reframe failure, develop mental toughness, and foster a survivor's mindset. Just like Uncle Buck stopped three feet from gold, many people give up when success is right around the corner. But the most resilient individuals push forward, reframe setbacks, and find meaning in their struggles.

Resilience isn't just a trait. It's a choice. The choice to keep digging. The choice to learn. And the choice to never quit before the breakthrough.

• • •

Viktor Frankl and Sara Blakely have very different stories but are great examples of embracing resilience. Ultimately, their stories prove that greatness comes not just from brilliance but from resilience and mastering the fundamentals.

To explore resources from this book, scan the QR code or visit RichByChoiceBook.com/bonus.

Nick and Chelsea's Resilience

The phone call shattered the peaceful rhythm of my golf trip like a thunderclap on a clear day. "We don't know what's wrong with her," Chelsea's voice trembled through the receiver, each syllable striking my chest like a hammer. My sweet Kinsley Blayke, my baby girl, my princess, was being rushed to the hospital.

Her body had turned a sickly yellow, her strength fading. The doctors, those meant to hold the answers, had none. I was miles away, stranded, helpless, trapped in a nightmare where distance was my greatest enemy. Every fiber of my being screamed to be by their side, but I had no way to get home.

Until, by God's grace, a friend's plane became my lifeline. The flight home was silent, my prayers the only sound in my heart. *Please, Lord, don't take her. Please, let me trade places. Please, just let her be okay.*

The next week inside the hospital walls was emotionally draining with fear, pain, and waiting. My little girl, just four years old, was poked, prodded, and drained of her innocence. Her cries echoed down the sterile hallways. Every two hours, another needle. Another test. Another moment of helplessness. And then came the words that crushed us—hemolytic anemia.

Hemolytic anemia is a disorder in which red blood cells are destroyed faster than they can be made. The destruction of red blood cells is called hemolysis. Without enough oxygen, your body can't work and begins to shut down. But the scarier part was the doctors did not know what was causing it.

Bad news turns into terrifying news; it's a condition so often linked to cancer. We were moved to the children's cancer unit. Walking through those doors was like stepping into the abyss of every parent's greatest fear. But even in that darkness, something unshakable rose within me. If I couldn't control the storm, I could anchor my family through it. I would not let this divide us. I would be the rock, the protector, the steady force in the chaos. My family and our future happiness were my "Who" and "Why."

There were another several days of imaging the worst, expecting the worst, sleepless nights, and sad days. Then, the miracle, the doctors returned with an answer that redefined relief: it wasn't cancer. It was a rare infection, curable, temporary, a battle we could win. That week changed me forever because I finally understood: Control is an illusion, but love, purpose, and gratitude... that is what remains unshaken.

As we walked out of the hospital, gratitude filled our hearts, but so did something else. A deep, aching awareness of the children we were leaving behind. Sadly, some would never get a chance to step outside those doors again. The warriors, the fighters, the kids who carried 100 times more courage in their tiny frames than I ever had on my best day. They weren't just battling sickness; they were fighting for their very lives.

It shook me to my core. What right did I have to complain? What struggle in my life could possibly compare? What challenge is so great that I cannot rise above it? What excuse do I have to let fear, frustration, or doubt hold me back? Maybe the worst day in my life isn't so bad after all. Maybe, just maybe, every challenge I face is an opportunity to grow, to fight, and to be grateful for every single breath.

7

Design by Choice
Create the Life You Want,
Not the Life You Have.

The Widower Who Rebuilt His Life

Marcus sat alone in the dim glow of the nightlight, listening to the soft, steady breath of his sleeping daughter. The silence in their home was deafening, a hollow echo of the love that once filled it. Cancer had taken his wife, Kathy, his best friend, the mother of his little girl Lilly, and in its wake, it left grief so heavy it threatened to pull him under.

But that night, as he knelt beside his beautiful daughter's bed, watching the way her tiny fingers clutched her favorite stuffed bunny, something inside him shifted. This wasn't just about survival—it was about *creating* something new, something beautiful out of the pain. He refused to let tragedy steal his daughter's future.

So, with tears still drying on his face, Marcus sat down at the kitchen table and wrote. Every detail, every hope, every dream—he mapped out the life his daughter *deserved*—a life filled with adventure, security, and love, a life where she never had to wonder if she was safe or if her father was present. That night, his vision became his purpose.

In the months that followed, Marcus threw himself into learning about investing, business, and financial independence. He worked tirelessly, not just to rebuild but to *reinvent* their lives. Late nights turned into small victories, and small victories became momentum.

Five years later, he stood on the porch of their dream home, watching his daughter race through the yard, her laughter ringing through the air like music. The pain of the past would always be a part of him, but it no longer defined him.

His vision—the one he wrote that night—was no longer just words on a page. It was their reality. He hadn't just built a future. He honored the love that was lost by creating something extraordinary for the love that remained.

Creating the Life You Want

By viewing money as a tool for creating a fulfilling life rather than a source of stress, we open ourselves up to a wonderful world of possibilities. This involves setting goals that align with your values, being kind to yourself during financial challenges, and celebrating every small victory along the way with loved ones.

You are worth it. Your loved ones are worth it. Your life has value beyond measure, and the love you hold for the people in your life is the very fuel that will carry you to the finish line. Let me tell you this: *You can have the life you want.* You can live a life of joy and fulfillment.

What defines a fulfilling and happy life is unique for each of us. It's not better or worse than someone else's—it's simply different. And that's beautiful. The ultimate goal is not to compare but to know, deep down, what will make *you* happy and design your life around that vision. As you're reading these words, I know you already have a sense of what that life looks like. You know your dreams, your desires, and your goals.

Harvard Business School conducted a study that shows that people who have clear, written goals and a plan to achieve them are far more successful.[46] In fact, the study revealed that the 3 percent of Harvard MBAs who wrote down their goals earned ten times as much as the other 97 percent combined.

The life you just dreamed of is not only possible, but it's *within reach.* It doesn't matter your age, income, or social status. So, let's tap into that power and complete an exercise together that can open the door to your best self. It's not only fun but incredibly insightful. This isn't just an activity; it's a chance to gain wisdom about the life you truly want to create.

First, I want you to stop for a moment. Find a comfortable place, take a deep breath, and close your eyes. Imagine a life where financial stress doesn't exist—a life where your finances are in harmony, and you never have to worry about money. Picture waking up without anxiety about bills or investments, a life free of worry about your family's financial future.

As you sit there, remain relaxed and calm, and take another deep breath. Let the air fill your lungs, and as you exhale, allow your mind to drift to a place of possibility. Can you see it? Can you picture the greatness your life could hold? Slowly, the image sharpens in your mind. You're there, surrounded by your family in a paradise, bathed in the warmth of love and joy. Focus on the scene—can you visualize the stunning colors that paint your surroundings? The sky above, the greenery around, and the brilliant blues of the water?

Let your mind soak in the details of the view. Can you feel the breeze against your skin, the warmth of the sun, the texture of the earth beneath your feet? Do you hear the sounds—the rustling of trees, the laughter of your loved ones, the hum of life surrounding you? Look around—can you see the pure joy on your family's faces, the happiness that radiates from their hearts?

Now, take this vision further. Picture your home, a place that brings peace and warmth to your family. Imagine your career, something that fills your soul with purpose and meaning. Hold that image close, and let it bring a smile to your face and a deep sense of fulfillment to your heart. How incredible is this life you are crafting in your mind?

Next, ask yourself, *What lights my soul on fire?* What is that one pursuit, that idea, that passion that ignites something deep within you, compelling you to move forward despite challenges? Let your mind wander and your heart guide you as you discover the spark that fuels your very existence—the thing that makes you feel most alive.

The next step is where your dream begins to take shape. Write it all down—every beautiful detail. Let your words capture the essence of what you want; don't stop until every vision is on the page. Be specific. Describe what brings you joy, what makes your heart sing. Write down what you see in your relationships—love, connection, growth. Detail the hobbies that excite you, the adventures you long to embark on, the places you dream of visiting, and the ways you wish to give back.

Imagine your home—its warmth and beauty. Picture the car you drive, the joy of new experiences with your family, and the laughter shared over exciting adventures. Dream about your retirement, filled with incredible moments, and write it all down, piece by piece. Imagine living every day with that fire burning brightly, propelling you toward your highest potential. What is it that calls to your soul, making your purpose undeniable? Find that fire, and let it illuminate your path forward.

Fill the page with your desires, no matter how big or small. Don't stop until you've painted the complete picture of your ideal life. The more detailed you are, the more vivid your future becomes. Let your words be your guide, leading you toward the life you truly desire.

What you've just written is more than a list; this is the roadmap to your unique version of financial freedom, the blueprint of your joyful life. It's your personal vision of ultimate happiness, a reflection of what *you* need to thrive, not what anyone else defines for you. This exercise is your first step toward understanding yourself on a deeper level.

You have the power to be Rich by Choice, to create a life of peace, joy, and financial happiness. The dreams you wrote down are not just fantasies but achievable realities. All you need is the right plan, the right mindset, and the determination to follow through. You *can* have the life you want. If you need to repeat this exercise, do so. I revisit this exercise yearly and follow it up with an action plan.

• • •

Becoming Rich by Choice looks different for everyone, and that's the beauty of it. It's not a one-size-fits-all destination but a life crafted around *your* values, dreams, and what brings you peace and joy. It's more than having enough to cover emergencies. It's the power to make choices without fear of financial consequences. It's the freedom to say, "Today, I can do whatever I want," without worry or hesitation. Imagine waking up every morning with that level of peace in your heart.

Beyond that, imagine how it feels to *give*—to bless others from a place of abundance. Picture helping a struggling family, providing for those who need it, or making a difference in the lives of children who wouldn't otherwise have gifts on Christmas morning. Rich by Choice is not just about living—it's about giving.

Money is always secondary to happiness. It has no real value unless used to enhance, protect, and bring joy to those you cherish most. True wealth is found in the moments, relationships, and dreams that fill your heart, not in a bank account balance. Most important is taking the time to deeply understand what will truly make you happy, what fuels your soul. Once you've discovered that, you can begin using money as the tool it was meant to be and turn those dreams into reality, creating a life filled with purpose, love, and fulfillment.

Designing the Life You Want

There are moments in life that redefine everything—our purpose, our motivation, and the way we see our future. For me, that moment came when my mentor introduced me to a simple but incredibly powerful exercise: *Creating My Vision Statement.*

The exercise had me create a deeply personal blueprint for the life I truly wanted to live. At its core, this exercise wasn't just about setting goals. It was about unlocking the deepest desires of my heart—all my hopes, dreams, and the things that would bring me the greatest joy.

I call it *The Rocking Chair Test*. Imagine yourself at 120 years old, sitting in a rocking chair, reflecting on your life. You're at peace, filled with gratitude. What had to happen—*specifically*—for you to lean back with a full heart and say, *"This was an amazing life"*? Not just *a good life*. Not just *an okay life*. But a life overflowing with joy, adventure, love, laughter, and unforgettable moments.

Here's how it works:

1. **Find a quiet space**—somewhere without distractions.
2. **Grab 10 blank sheets of paper, a pen, and a cold drink.**
3. **Give yourself an hour to dream—without limits.**

Write down everything that comes to mind:

- The dream homes that make your heart race
- The cars that bring you excitement
- The breathtaking vacations and adventures you long for
- The hobbies and passions that light you up
- The unforgettable experiences you want to create
- The deep, loving relationships you desire
- The perfect structure of your days—how you want to spend your time
- The things that bring you the most joy and fulfillment

Write freely. Write boldly. Don't hold back. If it crosses your mind—even for a second—put it on the page. This is *your* vision, *your* future, and *your* chance to design a life that excites you.

Vague dreams create vague results. Saying, *"I want freedom in retirement to have fun"* or *"I want to build my dream home"* is a great start, but don't stop there. Go deeper. Be specific. What does *freedom* look like to you? How do you spend your mornings, your afternoons, your nights? What makes your heart race with excitement?

Instead of just *dreaming* of a dream home, *build* it in your mind. Is it a cozy lakefront cabin with floor-to-ceiling windows where you watch the sunrise over the water? A beachside retreat with a sprawling wraparound porch where you sip coffee to the sound of crashing waves? Or a luxurious mountain lodge with a roaring fireplace, exposed wooden beams, and enough space for the entire family to gather for holidays?

The more details you pour onto the page, the more real your vision becomes. The more real it becomes, the greater the chance you'll make it happen. So write *with passion*. Write *without limits*. Because this isn't just an exercise—it's the first step to creating the extraordinary life you deserve. Below are a few examples to help you.

Mr. and Mrs. Smith:
The Retirement Hobbies That Fill Every Day with Joy

Mr. Smith

Retirement isn't about slowing down—it's about *finally* doing all the things that make my heart race with excitement. Mornings start on the golf course, walking the lush fairways as the sun rises, perfecting my swing, and competing in a friendly tournament with lifelong friends. In the afternoons, I dive into my woodworking shop, crafting beautiful hand-carved furniture for my kids and grandkids, knowing each piece will be treasured for generations. Twice a week, I gather with my band—yes, I'm finally learning guitar!—playing classic rock tunes just for fun.

And let's not forget about cooking. Every Friday, I host a legendary dinner party, experimenting with gourmet recipes, laughing with loved ones, and filling our home with the scent of rosemary, garlic, and sizzling steaks.

Mrs. Smith

This fabulous chapter in my life is about finally embracing the passions that fill my soul with joy. Mornings begin with a warm cup of coffee on the back porch, watching the sun rise over my flower garden, the air rich with the scent of jasmine and fresh earth. Twice a week, I meet my best friends for a lively round of pickleball, where the competition is fierce but the laughter is even louder.

In the afternoons, I retreat to my cozy craft room, where I quilt intricate family heirlooms; each stitch is a love letter to my kids and grandkids. Some days, I spend hours in my sun-drenched art studio, painting vibrant landscapes that remind me of my favorite travels. On other afternoons, I can be found in my book nook, curled up with a novel that whisks me away to another world.

A few times a week, I meet my group of incredible women for brunch at our favorite café, where we sip lavender lattes, swap stories, and plan our next big adventure—whether it's a group cruise, a weekend getaway to a charming mountain town, or simply an afternoon of antique shopping. We've also started a monthly wine and wisdom night, where we gather in someone's home, share our favorite bottle of wine, and dive into deep, meaningful conversations about life, family, and the joys of this chapter.

Every Friday, my kitchen becomes the heart of the home. I bake homemade pies, knead fresh bread, and prepare my famous Sunday sauce—because nothing brings people together like a home-cooked meal. The house fills with the scent of cinnamon and roasted garlic as I welcome family and friends for our weekly dinner gathering, where stories are shared, laughter echoes, and memories are made.

And, of course, there's music. Once a week, I gather with my women's choir, harmonizing old jazz classics and Broadway tunes, proving that passion has no age limit.

This is the retirement I dreamed of—full of creativity, connection, and the freedom to savor every beautiful moment.

Coy and Terri: Staying Connected with Kids & Grandkids

Our family is the heartbeat of our lives. We fly to visit the kids and grandkids at least four times a year—spending every holiday together, making Christmas mornings magical, filling the house with laughter and excitement. But we go beyond visits—we create traditions.

Every summer, we rent a massive lake house where the entire family gathers, filled with boat rides, water balloon fights, s'mores by the fire, and unforgettable memories. We also host "Grandparent Camp" every July, where the grandkids stay with us for a week of storytelling, scavenger hunts, movie nights, and homemade pancake breakfasts.

Zack and Amy: The Ultimate Dream Home

Our dream home is a sanctuary—a place where love, laughter, and comfort fill every room. Nestled on 10 acres just outside of town, it's a sprawling farmhouse with a wraparound porch, a porch swing that creaks gently in the breeze, and bright yellow shutters that make it feel warm and welcoming. Inside, the open-concept kitchen is the heart of the home, with a massive island perfect for gathering around while cooking up holiday feasts. The living room boasts towering stone fireplaces, oversized leather chairs, and family photos lining the walls. The backyard? An oasis. A pool with a rock waterfall, an outdoor kitchen with a wood-fired pizza oven, and a barn-turned-guesthouse for when family visits.

Stacy and Jim: Volunteering That Fills the Soul

Giving back is a non-negotiable part of our lives. We dedicate every Tuesday to mentoring young entrepreneurs, helping them turn their dreams into reality. Twice a month, we serve at a local food pantry, not just handing out meals but sitting and listening—truly listening—to the stories of those who need encouragement. We fund scholarships for kids who dream of college but lack the means. Once a year, we embark on a mission trip, building homes for families in need and experiencing the joy of making a tangible difference.

Now, It's Your Turn.

What does your dream life look like? Write it down. Be specific. Dream boldly. The more detailed your vision, the more powerful it becomes.

This is your life's masterpiece. Your *vision*. Write it boldly, dream bigger than ever, and give yourself permission to craft a life that truly excites you. Because one day, when you're in that rocking chair looking back, you deserve to smile, knowing you *lived fully, loved deeply, and left nothing undone.*

You are worth it. Your loved ones are worth it. Your life has value beyond measure, and the love you hold for the people in your life is the very fuel that will carry you to the finish line. Let me tell you this: *You can have the life you want.* You can live a life of joy and fulfillment.

To explore resources from this book, scan the QR code or visit RichByChoiceBook.com/bonus.

Nick and Chelsea's Design

The Moment It Became Real

After I completed my design, something incredible happened. I came home one evening and found Chelsea working on hers. I hadn't even asked her to do it—she just saw how much fun I was having and wanted to experience it, too. That's the kind of person she is.

The next step? We each went back through our lists and circled the things that mattered most. For example, a couple I once worked with wrote down *his and her Mercedes*—which sounded fun! But when they reflected on what truly mattered, they realized that while it would be nice, they weren't willing to work extra years to achieve it.

Then, Chelsea and I did something even more powerful. We reviewed each other's lists together. We laughed. We dreamed. We discovered so many things we had in common and were also surprised by the things that were uniquely ours. This simple exercise deepened our relationship. It gave us a fresh appreciation for each other's dreams, future desires, and goals.

The Transformation

Before this, budgeting, saving, and investing money felt like a chore. It was just another task, another responsibility. But after completing our vision statements, everything changed. Now, every dollar we saved had a purpose. Every financial decision became a step toward something we were *excited* about.

Chelsea and I weren't just saving—we were *building*. Together.

A vision isn't just a dream; it's a destination. And once you know where you're going, the journey becomes thrilling. This exercise didn't just change my outlook—it changed my future. It turned planning into passion, money into meaning, and dreams into something tangible.

And now, I invite you to do the same. Your *amazing* life starts with a vision. What will yours look like?

8

Awareness by Choice
Realization Unlocks Opportunity.

Who Are They?

Person 1: This woman grew up in poverty and faced numerous personal struggles early in life. However, she soon realized her greatest strength was his ability to connect with people on an emotional level. She leveraged her natural empathy and communication skills to become a media mogul, transforming how people engage with television and personal growth. At the same time, she understood her weakness was having an impulsive nature around business decisions, so she surrounded herself with trusted advisors and experts who helped guide her business empire. By playing to her strengths and protecting against her weaknesses, she created one of the most successful media brands in the world.

Answer: She is Oprah Winfrey, with an estimated net worth of around $3.5 billion.

Person 2: They are both renowned for their brilliance and share a powerful drive to revolutionize industries. They are visionaries, constantly pushing boundaries and taking innovation to unthinkable heights. Their relentless pursuit of perfection is their greatest strength, yet it is also their greatest weakness. In the early stages of their careers, they were both known for their impatience. Their demand for excellence strained relationships. Though their ideas have been groundbreaking, they struggled with the human side of leadership, often alienating team members. Over time, they each came to a crucial realization: They couldn't succeed alone. They had to acknowledge their weaknesses and complement them with the strengths of others. For one, it meant stepping back from day-to-day management; for the other, it meant delegating operational responsibilities.

Answer: Steve Jobs and Elon Musk serve as reminders that even the most brilliant minds can achieve far more by understanding and addressing their strengths and weaknesses.

Person 3: When he reflects on his journey, he sees how his leadership brought immense strength to the fight against apartheid. However, he also recognizes that his passion sometimes leads to impulsive decisions. Spending 27 years in prison gave him the time to truly understand himself. Through this period of reflection, he learned the importance of patience and self-awareness. He emerged not with anger but with a renewed sense of purpose. He once said, "I learned that courage was not the absence of fear, but the triumph over it."

Understanding his strengths and weaknesses allowed him to maximize his strengths and develop strategies to protect himself from his shortcomings. He knew wisdom and empathy, even for his enemies, were crucial to leading South Africa into a new era. While he could inspire millions, he also knew governance required different skills. He leaned on trusted advisors to handle the intricacies of leadership, allowing him to focus on uniting people.

By leveraging his strengths and acknowledging where he needed support, he was able to guide South Africa's peaceful transition. This collaboration, built on trust and understanding, allowed him to become not just a leader but a symbol of peace and reconciliation.

Answer: He is Nelson Mandela, a freedom fighter who endured 27 years of imprisonment and emerged to transform a nation and the entire world. Mandela's legacy is a global symbol of peace, justice, courage, and compassion.

The lesson here is powerful. Self-awareness and resilience are the foundations of success. When people take the time to truly understand their strengths and weaknesses and desire to rise above what holds them back, they can craft strategies that help them reach their potential and design the life they want. That balance—between what they're good at and where they need to improve—leads to true greatness.

The Key to Unlocking Your Potential

You are uniquely and wonderfully made, with strengths that empower you and weaknesses that shape your journey. Instead of wishing you were someone else, embrace exactly who you are, because understanding yourself is the key to unlocking your full potential. When you recognize your natural strengths, you can build upon them; when you acknowledge your weaknesses, you can protect yourself from them. But how does this connect to money? In every way imaginable. The way you think, feel, and behave—your psychology—directly influences your financial decisions, your relationship with money, and, ultimately, your ability to create a life of fulfillment and freedom.

Understanding yourself is the key to unlocking your full potential.

Sarah and Mark are two individuals with very different approaches to money, yet both are equally unhappy. Sarah was a natural saver, meticulously putting aside every extra dollar she earned. She lived with financial security but rarely enjoyed the fruits of her hard work. Vacations, dinners out, or even small indulgences were rare because she feared spending would undo all her careful planning. Over time, she realized she wasn't experiencing life—her focus on saving had created a rigid, joyless, and unfulfilling life.

On the other hand, there was Mark. Mark loved to spend, believing that life was meant to be enjoyed in the moment. He took trips, dined out frequently, and was always ready to buy the latest gadget or experience. But with each purchase came a lingering anxiety. He was constantly stressed about bills, unsure how to cover the next expense. His financial situation brought him sleepless nights, and the joy he got from spending was short-lived, quickly replaced by worry and regret.

Both Sarah and Mark were missing something vital. It wasn't that one was better or worse than the other. Sarah's strength was in her discipline, but she needed balance to enjoy the life she worked so hard to secure. Mark's strength was in living fully, but he needed boundaries to ensure his enjoyment didn't lead to financial chaos. The goal for both wasn't to change who they were but to understand themselves better—to recognize their strengths and weaknesses with money and find harmony.

The key for Sarah and Mark was simple: maximize their strengths while protecting themselves from their weaknesses. For Sarah, that meant allowing herself to spend on what brought joy, guilt-free. For Mark, it meant learning how to save in a way that didn't stifle his zest for life but gave him the peace of mind to enjoy it fully.

Ultimately, both found happiness not by changing who they were but by choosing to be aware of how to use their natural tendencies in a way that allowed them to thrive.

Know Thyself

In 400 B.C., the Greek philosopher Socrates stated that the key to human advancement could be expressed in two simple words: "Know thyself." So I ask you: Do you know yourself? Truly, deeply, do you know your financial self?

You might be thinking, "Of course, I know myself. I know what I like, what I don't like, what I want, and what I don't want. What does this have to do with my finances?" I'm glad you asked because it has everything to do with your financial life. Most people think they want more money, maybe to become millionaires, but that's often where their self-awareness stops. Sure, you might know what's in your bank account or retirement fund, but have you ever questioned why you think about money the way you do?

"Knowing yourself is the beginning of all wisdom," Aristotle once said. It's more than understanding your bank balance; it's about understanding the psychology behind your financial choices. By the end of this chapter, you will be able to answer these questions about yourself:

- What are your **Money Strengths?**
- What are your **Money Weaknesses?**
- What is your **Money Psychology?**

Recognizing these can make all the difference between a life of financial peace and a life of financial strain.

Money Strengths and Weaknesses

One of the most critical aspects of financial self-awareness is understanding your Money Strengths and Weaknesses. Like Mark and Sarah, if you know where your strengths lie, you can use them to your advantage. If you understand your weaknesses, you can plan around them and make adjustments to protect yourself from potential pitfalls.

Everyone has strengths and weaknesses, and that's okay. You're not flawed; you're human. What's important is being aware of them, especially when it comes to your finances and relationships.

Many of us have been taught that being a saver is inherently better than being a spender. Savers are virtuous, and spenders are reckless. We hear things like, "My spouse is the spender in the family," as if that's a flaw. But I'm here to tell you that neither being a natural saver nor a natural spender makes you better or worse. Yes, saving is good, but spending wisely is also important. Whether you're a natural saver or a natural spender, you have unique strengths and weaknesses; the goal is to understand them.

For example, natural savers are often disciplined with money and skilled at saving for retirement, avoiding debt, and planning for the future. However, they might struggle with generosity or enjoying the present. On the other hand, natural spenders tend to be generous, living in the moment and enjoying life, but they often face challenges with saving and debt management. Both types have strengths and areas for growth.

The key to financial growth lies in knowing yourself. Identifying your strengths and weaknesses allows you to maximize your strengths, all while developing systems to protect you against your weaknesses. This mindful approach ensures that your financial decisions are not just reactive but thoughtful and forward-looking.

The key to financial growth lies in knowing yourself.

Spender or Saver? A Quick Quiz

This 5-question multiple-choice quiz will help you determine if you are a natural saver or spender. Each question includes an explanation to help you understand your tendencies based on your answers.

1. How do you feel when you receive unexpected money (like a bonus or gift)?

   A. Excited to spend it on something I've been wanting.

B. I think about saving it for the future.

C. I split it between saving and spending.

Explanation:

A. You might be a natural spender if your first thought is to spend immediately. Spenders often get more enjoyment from using money in the moment.

B. Natural savers prioritize building their financial security and find comfort in saving, even with unexpected funds.

C. If you split between the two, you may take a balanced approach, enjoying your money now while still preparing for the future.

2. What do you do when you're out shopping and see something you like that's not on your list?

A. I usually buy it, even if I hadn't planned on it.

B. I stick to my list and avoid impulse purchases.

C. I might consider it, but I'll think it over before deciding.

Explanation:

A. Spontaneous purchasing is a classic trait of a natural spender. You likely value the immediate satisfaction money can bring.

B. If you stick to your list, you may be a natural saver who carefully plans and controls where your money goes.

C. Thinking it over suggests you have tendencies of both—a spender's interest and a saver's caution.

3. How do you feel about budgeting and tracking your spending?

A. It feels too restrictive—I prefer to be flexible with my money.

B. I find it important and try to stick to a strict budget.

C. I like the idea of budgeting, but I'm not super strict with it.

Explanation:

A. Avoiding budgets could indicate you're more of a natural spender, enjoying the freedom of not being tied to strict financial plans.

B. If you stick to a budget, you likely have a natural saver mindset. Savers value organization and long-term planning.

C. A moderate approach shows you might appreciate the structure but also want room for enjoyment.

4. If you need to make a big purchase (like a car or vacation), what's your approach?

   A. I'm willing to go into debt or take out a loan to afford it right away.
   B. I'd save up for it and wait until I could pay in full.
   C. I might finance part of it, but I aim to pay it off quickly.

   Explanation:

   A. Being willing to take on debt suggests you might be more focused on enjoying money in the present, which is characteristic of a spender.
   B. Waiting until you've saved the full amount is a trait of a natural saver, preferring financial stability over immediate gratification.
   C. Combining both strategies suggests a practical mindset—you're willing to enjoy spending but prefer not to let debt linger.

5. What's your general approach to long-term financial goals, like retirement or emergency savings?

   A. I'll think about that later; there's plenty of time to save.
   B. I actively contribute to long-term savings and make it a priority.
   C. I'm aware of the need for it but haven't been as consistent as I should.

Explanation:

A. If long-term savings aren't your priority now, it might indicate you're a natural spender focusing more on short-term enjoyment.

B. Actively contributing to savings shows the disciplined mindset of a natural saver who prioritizes future security.

C. If you're aware but not fully consistent, it suggests a balanced approach—you may want to save but find it challenging at times to stick to it.

Scoring Guide:

- Mostly A's: You lean toward being a natural spender. You enjoy the present and prefer to use your money for experiences or purchases that bring immediate happiness.

- Mostly B's: You're likely a natural saver with a strong focus on long-term security and financial stability.

- Mostly C's: You fall somewhere in between, demonstrating both spending and saving tendencies. You likely value balance, enjoying some of your money now while preparing for the future.

This quiz helps identify your natural tendencies, but remember, both saving and spending can be managed in a way that leads to financial success when appropriately balanced.

A Practical Path Forward

If you're a natural saver, focus on improving areas where you struggle. For example, you could set up an automatic system where a portion of your income goes toward giving or fun, forcing yourself to spend on things that bring joy or help others. Meanwhile, natural spenders can benefit from making savings, debt reduction, investing, and all financial planning... automatic. The goal is to understand strengths, weaknesses, and money psychology. Not to beat themselves up and dwell on their past mistakes and life:

There is a quiet brilliance inside you, shaped by your experiences, and you don't need to be "fixed." Growth comes not from perfection but from progress. Mistakes and setbacks are not failures—they are lessons, proof that you're on the path of growth and discovery. Be kind to yourself, embrace the progress you are going to make, and be excited about your future.

Remember: Our lives are not defined by what happens to us; our lives are ultimately defined by how we react to what happens to us.

Rich the EASY Way[IP]

Building wealth doesn't have to be complicated, stressful, or overwhelming. I want to help you become Rich the EASY Way. With the right strategy, success can be **Effortless, Automated, Systemized, and Designed for You**—the *E.A.S.Y.* way. Imagine a financial future where your money grows on autopilot, your investments work smarter (not harder), and your path to wealth feels simple, natural, and completely within reach. Rich the EASY Way is about leveraging proven systems, making intelligent decisions, and creating a life of financial freedom—without the struggle. How? Make AUTOMATION your new best friend. E.A.S.Y is how you turn your weaknesses into strengths.

E.A.S.Y. – *Effortless Automation, Systemized for You*

- Effortless
- Automation
- Systemized
- You

Mark and Sarah Thompson are a humble, hardworking couple whose inspiring journey to financial peace showcases the power of simplicity and discipline. Together, they decided to be Rich by Choice. Mark worked as a schoolteacher, earning about $42,000 a year, and Sarah was a part-time nurse, making no more than $50,000 annually. Despite their modest combined income, they accomplished what many only dream of: they paid off two homes, funded their two children's college educations without debt, and retired at 54 with a net worth of $2.1 million.

Their success wasn't the result of a lucky break or a family inheritance. Instead, it came from a simple yet powerful decision they made together early in their marriage: to make their financial future automatic. From their very first paycheck as newlyweds, Mark and Sarah embraced a "pay yourself first" philosophy, setting up automatic contributions to retirement and investment accounts before they touched a single penny for bills or discretionary spending. They didn't have to stress over making the right decision each month; their future was taken care of before they even had a chance to second-guess themselves. Can you imagine that peace in your life?

Yet, their approach wasn't just about saving and investing. One of the Thompsons' most fulfilling decisions was to make their giving automatic too. From the start, they arranged to donate a percentage of their income every month to local charities and their church. "We wanted to give joyfully, not out of guilt or obligation," Sarah shared. "And by making it automatic, we ensured that giving was always a part of our lives, even during lean years." They found deep fulfillment knowing that their contributions helped fund scholarships for underprivileged kids and supported their community's food bank.

They also chose a 15-year mortgage on their home, ensuring that by the time their children were in high school, they owned their house outright. With the freed-up cash flow, they invested in a modest rental property that eventually became another source of passive income. By the time they retired, the income from their investments was more than enough to sustain them. What brought them the most joy, though, wasn't just their financial independence—it was the knowledge that they had given their children a head start in life. Both of their kids graduated from college debt-free, giving them the freedom to chase their dreams without the burden of student loans.

"When we saw our daughter walk across that graduation stage," Mark said with a tear in his eye, "we realized that all those years of discipline weren't just about us. They were about creating a legacy of opportunity."

The Thompsons' story is a testament to the idea that financial peace isn't reserved for high earners or the exceptionally gifted. With consistency, automation, and a heart for giving, anyone can achieve a life of financial joy, security, and significance. Mark and Sarah's journey reminds us that wealth is more than numbers in a bank account—it's the choice we all have to use money to create a life filled with meaning, purpose, and lasting fulfillment.

Being aware of who you are financially is the foundation for lasting success. As Oprah Winfrey once said, "When you know better, you do better." By taking the time to reflect on your money strengths and weaknesses, you can formulate a plan that works for your goals and enhances your life. After all, the goal isn't just wealth; it's a life well-lived.

Take time to understand who you are, your money strengths, and your money weaknesses. Once you do, you'll be better equipped to make decisions that bring you financial peace, joy, and purpose.

Your Money Psychology: Understanding Ourselves and Others

A remarkable story illustrates how, once you take the time to understand someone's past, what once seemed irrational or "crazy" suddenly makes sense. Take Howard Schultz, the visionary former CEO of Starbucks. From the outside, some might see Schultz's business decisions—like offering healthcare to part-time workers or giving employees stock options—as overly generous and even impractical in the cutthroat business world. But to truly understand Schultz's choices, you have to look at his roots.

Schultz grew up in a working-class family in the Brooklyn projects. His father held numerous low-paying jobs without job security, benefits, or healthcare. When Schultz was just seven years old, his father broke his ankle on the job and was laid off without compensation or medical support.

That moment stuck with him. Years later, as Schultz built Starbucks into a global empire, he made it a mission to treat his employees, whom he calls "partners," with the dignity his father never received.

"When you're growing up in an environment where you're constantly faced with the inequities of life, you ask yourself, 'Why not me?'" Schultz once said, reflecting on his journey. This mindset propelled him to create a company culture that prioritizes the well-being of its workers. Today, Starbucks provides healthcare benefits to hundreds of thousands of employees, including part-time staff, a decision that has cost the company hundreds of millions of dollars but has also built immense loyalty and a positive work environment.

Schultz's vision didn't stop there. He also introduced the Starbucks College Achievement Plan, which offers employees free college tuition through Arizona State University's online program.

Some critics might have thought these initiatives were financially unsound, but for Schultz, they were personal. "Success is best when it's shared," he famously said, emphasizing that the health and future of his employees were integral to the company's long-term success. What some saw as "crazy generosity" was, in Schultz's eyes, a path to sustainable growth rooted in compassion.

Howard Schultz's story is a powerful reminder that a person's actions make perfect sense when seen through the lens of their past. What appears unconventional, impractical, or even "crazy" often stems from deeply personal experiences. Schultz's decisions at Starbucks were not just about business; they were about changing lives—something he knew all too well from his upbringing.

People Are Not Crazy

We aren't crazy, even if we sometimes do questionable things with money. In reality, we are shaped by a complex web of experiences, and understanding this is key to unlocking our financial habits. Think about it—each of us comes from a unique background, shaped by our upbringing, the economic environment we grew up in, and the values instilled in us. These influences shape how we view the world, particularly regarding finances. What might seem illogical or "silly" to one person can make perfect sense to someone else.

Consider the differences between someone raised during the Great Depression of the 1930s and someone who came of age in the economic boom of the 1990s. One learned that survival meant hoarding every penny, preparing for the worst because it could all disappear tomorrow. The other might view risk and spending through a lens of abundance, believing that opportunity was always just around the corner. These differing worldviews are not random; they are ingrained responses to the environments in which these individuals were raised.

And it's not just generational. Imagine two people growing up in the same neighborhood but in very different financial realities. One person may have been raised in wealth, viewing money as a tool for growth and freedom. Meanwhile, just a few streets over, another person might have experienced poverty, where money was elusive, a source of stress, and often out of reach. Both have entirely different relationships with finances despite their proximity, and those early experiences shape the rest of their lives.

Now, let's take it deeper. Maybe you knew someone who saved everything but never indulged in life's pleasures, always focused on the future, only to pass away before they could enjoy the fruits of their labor. Because of that, you might see no point in saving, valuing the present over a distant future. Or maybe you've watched someone who lived for today, spending every dollar they earned, only to end up with nothing but regret. These stories anchor our financial beliefs, for better or worse.

Awareness of Yourself and Others

I once knew this newly married couple, radiating the joy of the honeymoon phase, blissfully claiming they never fought. But as we all know, no honeymoon lasts forever. Their first conflict was just around the corner, and it caught them off guard.

Linda loved the comforting hum of the television as she drifted to sleep—it was her nightly ritual. On the other hand, Stephen craved silence, the kind that allowed him to ease into a peaceful slumber. Every night, he waited patiently for Linda to fall asleep, then carefully switched off the TV so he could finally rest. He didn't want to stir any tension, so he kept his discomfort to himself. But when Stephen's work schedule changed, forcing him to rise earlier each morning, the dynamic shifted dramatically.

What had once been a quiet frustration grew into an ever-present irritant. Stephen began to feel like Linda's needs were overshadowing his own. *"How selfish can she be?"* he thought. After all, he contributed equally to the bills; shouldn't his preferences matter just as much? The frustration festered inside him, and soon, small annoyances blossomed into deeper resentment. Stephen became snappy, irritated, and distant, almost at the breaking point, questioning whether he could continue living this way.

Linda, too, noticed the change in him. The man she fell in love with—so kind, easygoing, and full of life—seemed to vanish before her eyes. Confused, she asked him what was wrong, only to be met with the dreaded "I'm fine." She didn't know what had changed, but the tension kept building.

Then came the explosion. Exhausted and fed up, Stephen finally let it out: "This marriage isn't working. I can't live like this anymore." Linda was floored. She didn't see this coming and had no idea what was truly bothering him.

It wasn't until they finally talked—really talked—that the deeper layers of Linda's needs were uncovered. She opened up about her childhood: an only child raised by a single mother working three jobs. Linda was often left to cope with the loneliness of an empty home. The TV had been her one companion. When it would break and there was no money to fix it, she sank into depression, swallowed by the silence. "My childhood was lonely and horrible," Linda explained softly, revealing a vulnerability that Stephen had never seen before. His heart sank as he finally understood what Linda had been holding onto all these years.

At that moment, everything changed. Stephen realized this wasn't about a television or falling asleep. It was about the scars Linda carried and the quiet battles she had fought long before they met.

It's incredible how a moment of compassionate listening, of genuine understanding, can shift everything. We are all imperfect people navigating an imperfect world. The goal is understanding—truly seeing each other for who we are and why we think and feel the way we do. Once we reach that place of understanding, solutions often appear with surprising simplicity. For Stephen and Linda, it was as easy as setting a sleep timer on the TV—a simple compromise that neither had seen through the fog of frustration.

The environments we grew up in undeniably influence our thoughts, feelings, and behaviors around money. But this doesn't mean we are irrational or trapped by our pasts. It simply means that we've been shaped by a lifetime of experiences.

Awareness by Choice Exercise

Take time to journal the following prompts. By answering these questions, you can better understand your personal Money Strengths, Weaknesses, and Psychology, and how your life experiences shape your current financial mindset and behaviors. Understanding this will help lead you on a path to an incredible life of Financial Happiness and being Rich by Choice.

1. **What early memories do I have about money, and how did they shape my current financial habits?** Reflect on how childhood experiences—whether witnessing abundance, scarcity, or financial insecurity—have influenced how you handle money today.

2. **What are my strongest skills in managing money, and how can I leverage them more effectively?** Identify areas where you naturally excel, such as saving, investing, or budgeting, and consider how to make those strengths even more impactful.

3. **In what financial situations do I feel the most stressed or vulnerable, and what patterns can I identify?** This question will help you recognize potential weaknesses, whether impulse spending, fear of investing, or avoidance of financial planning.

4. **How did my parents or caregivers view and manage money, and how has that shaped my financial**

behaviors? Understanding your inherited financial values can help you see where you may need to shift your mindset or reinforce healthy habits.

5. **What financial mistakes have I made, and what lessons did I take from them?** This allows you to reflect on your growth and how past failures have shaped your current approach to money management.

6. **Do I focus more on short-term financial goals (like spending for today) or long-term goals (like saving for the future)?** By identifying your natural tendency, you can develop a more balanced approach that aligns with your overall financial happiness.

7. **When I think about money, do I feel empowered or anxious, and what specific beliefs contribute to these feelings?** This question will help you uncover the emotional and psychological drivers behind your financial decisions.

8. **How do I define financial success, and how does that align with my personal values and life goals?** Understanding what financial success looks like for you, beyond just numbers, will help you align your financial habits with your broader life aspirations.

9. **What financial behaviors in others frustrate or confuse me, and what does that reveal about my own money beliefs?** Your reactions to others' financial decisions can be a mirror for your own biases, helping you uncover hidden beliefs about money.

10. **What steps can I take to better align my financial actions with my strengths while protecting myself from my weaknesses?** This question will guide you toward creating strategies that maximize your strengths—whether it's systematic savings or

disciplined investing—while safeguarding areas where you might struggle, like impulse spending or financial avoidance.

● ● ●

Understanding your personal money strengths, weaknesses, and the underlying psychology that drives your financial behavior is an incredibly empowering journey. By taking the time to reflect on your relationship with money, you can uncover why you make certain financial decisions and how past experiences have shaped your habits. This awareness doesn't just help you avoid pitfalls; it also allows you to harness your natural strengths—whether it's discipline in saving, a knack for investing, or an intuitive approach to budgeting—and use them to your advantage.

There is a quiet brilliance inside you, shaped by your experiences, and you don't need to be "fixed." Growth comes not from perfection but from progress. Mistakes and setbacks are not failures—they are lessons, proof that you're on the path of growth and discovery. Be kind to yourself, embrace the progress you are going to make, and be excited about your future.

Answering deeply insightful questions about your financial habits can bring clarity to areas where you might be vulnerable. Everyone has weaknesses, whether it's impulsive spending, avoidance of financial planning, or being overly cautious. However, understanding these vulnerabilities is the key to putting protective strategies in place.

By taking the time to explore these critical aspects of your financial life, you give yourself the gift of awareness—an awareness that leads to smarter, more intentional decisions. When you fully understand why you do what you do with money, you open the door to true financial empowerment and greater harmony in your relationship with wealth.

To explore resources from this book, scan the QR code or visit RichByChoiceBook.com/bonus.

Nick and Chelsea's Awareness Mindset

For my wife, Chelsea, and me, finances have always been a reflection of our distinct personalities. One of us is a natural spender, the other a natural saver. (I'll leave it to you to guess which is which!) But instead of allowing these differences to create tension, we've learned to work together toward our long-term financial goals. The way we've improved our personal finances is through a simple yet powerful system: automation.

We've made everything systematic. From the moment money enters our account, it's allocated automatically toward funding our goals. This includes everything from savings and retirement to investments, giving, and, yes, bills. But it doesn't stop there. We also allocate a set amount for fun and travel, a category that often gets overlooked. Here's the key: we don't just budget for fun; we *require* ourselves to spend it. This ensures we prioritize quality time as a family, making memories and nurturing our relationship.

Our system isn't just a financial plan—it's a strategy that allows both the spender and the saver in our relationship to thrive. We've struck a balance that honors both perspectives, enhancing our strengths and safeguarding us from our weaknesses. It's an approach that fosters joy, eliminates stress, and keeps us aligned on the path toward our dreams.

I highly recommend creating a system like this for yourself. It not only simplifies the process but also makes financial planning something that strengthens your relationship rather than strains it.

9

Faith by Choice
Embrace Timeless Wisdom to
Create Modern Solutions.

Dear Reader,

This chapter will contain much information about how my faith has positively impacted my life in a wonderful way. If you believe something different, I want you to know that I care about you and want to help you better your life.

Right now, through your personal life's journey, you might not believe everything in the Bible, or you tried "the church thing" and encountered a less-than-positive experience. You are not alone, you are welcome here, and please keep reading. You have made so much progress.

I want you to know that my desire to help and support you is not contingent upon your beliefs. While my own faith holds a significant place in my life, I deeply respect you and your beliefs.

My goal is to encourage, equip, and empower you with the proper tools, insights, and know-how to take charge of your life where your finances contribute to your happiness rather than distract you from it. By viewing money as a tool for creating a fulfilling life rather than a source of stress, we open ourselves up to a wonderful world of possibilities. Financial Happiness is not a distant dream; it's a living, breathing reality we can all embrace together.

God Bless,
Nick

The Journey to Truth:
Discovering the Secrets to Wealth and Happiness

Some journeys begin with a spark—an unexpected moment of revelation that sets a new course in life. Mine began in church, sitting in the right pews while my pastor, Pastor Rick, launched a series called "What the Bible Does Not Say." For several months, week after week, he uncovered truths hidden in plain sight.

He challenged widely held beliefs, exposing teachings that many assumed were biblical but weren't. It wasn't just fascinating—it was revolutionary. I realized how much I thought I knew about the Bible, but didn't.

It made me question: How much of what we believe about the Bible is rooted in tradition or assumption rather than truth? Have we been following ideas we think are scriptural without ever verifying them for ourselves? How much of what I believe is based only on what I have been told? These questions stirred something deep within me. I was captivated. And so, with my curiosity ignited, I embarked on what would become a life-changing journey.

Every morning, I opened the Bible, its pages becoming my daily companion. What began as curiosity quickly grew into unwavering commitment. With each passing day, the words took root in my heart and mind, gently reshaping my thoughts, actions, and the way I saw the world. I still begin every morning with its wisdom, not out of obligation, but because it feeds my soul, offering clarity, strength, and purpose.

I'll be the first to admit—I'm no Bible scholar, and I am far from perfect. But here's what I do know: there is an incredible sense of peace when you begin to truly understand your beliefs and live in alignment with them. It's not about perfection—it's about growth. It's about educating yourself, thinking critically, and not blindly accepting everything you've been told as absolute truth.

True joy and peace come when your life is in alignment. When the values you hold deep in your heart match the way you live. It's an incredible feeling knowing that your life and your heart are moving in the same direction. When your actions reflect the deepest truths of your heart, life flows effortlessly. Life will not be perfect, but joy becomes a more natural state, not a pursuit, in the quiet moments and the grand adventures alike.

The real transformation comes when you stop living on borrowed convictions and start discovering the truth for yourself. That's when life shifts—when faith becomes real, personal, and powerful. I would highly encourage you to begin your own journey. It will change your life. It changed mine in a wonderful way.

A Monumental Educational Quest

But my exploration didn't stop with Scripture. Coincidently, this was right at the peak of my pursuit of advanced education and elite certifications. I delved into hundreds of books and immersed myself in the wisdom of the world's brightest minds. I studied the lives of world leaders, visionary CEOs, innovators, philanthropists, and history-makers—people who shaped nations and left legacies. As I read their words and dissected their success stories, something remarkable happened: patterns began to emerge.

At first, they were subtle—just faint echoes of familiar ideas. But the more I read, the more those echoes became unmistakable harmonies. The core lessons and principles these titans of success followed weren't new or unique. They were ancient truths, repeated across centuries, cultures, and industries. And the more I compared their teachings to what I had been reading in the Bible, the more one thing became clear: The world's most successful people were knowingly following biblical principles… or unknowingly.

The Formula for Sustainable Wealth and Happiness

A thorough knowledge of the Bible is
worth more than a college education.
—Theodore Roosevelt

We often think wealth and happiness result from luck, talent, or being in the right place at the right time. But that's not the truth. Sustainable wealth and happiness do not happen by accident. Behind every great achievement lies a formula—a blueprint of habits, mindsets, and principles that are universally applicable.

> **Sustainable wealth and happiness do not happen by accident.**

Success leaves clues, and those clues often point us back to the same foundational truths. Our lives are not determined by what happens to us but by how we respond. Our actions and habits shape our destiny.

Daily choices become habits. Habits become the foundation of our future. *Good intentions are not enough.* You can have the best intentions in the world, but if they are built on the wrong habits, they will lead to failure. And unfortunately, too many people learn this lesson the hard way.

In America today, the statistics are grim: debt, financial stress, and poor money management are rampant. People are struggling not because they lack opportunities but because they lack the right habits. They are building their financial futures on shaky ground, and the cracks are beginning to show.

The Secrets of the Rich and Wealthy

So, what are the secrets of those who have achieved extraordinary success and wealth? The answer is simpler than you might think. These secrets are not hidden. They have been used for thousands of years and have never failed. The reason? They are rooted in timeless, biblical truths. I call these "The Fundamentals of Money."

Six Fundamentals of Money

• Positive Growth Mindset	• Budgeting and Planning
• Giving	• Saving and Investing
• Earning	• Spending

Mastering the Fundamentals of Money is essential to achieving true Financial Happiness and becoming Rich by Choice. These are not hidden secrets. No, these principles are timeless truths I stumbled upon.

The Fundamentals of Money are not mine. They are all from God. There is no need to reinvent the wheel. The same fundamentals that guided John D. Rockefeller, Warren Buffett, Henry Ford, and countless others are available to everyone, and they're found in the all-time greatest money book: The Bible.

Did you know that the Greek word "blessed" means "happy"? To have a blessed life, which scriptures state is available to everyone, is to have a happy life. These "secrets" will change your life forever.

The Bible is the greatest "Money Book" ever written. The secrets to wealth and happiness are hidden in plain sight, like a thread, woven throughout the text of the Bible. It is the best money guide for which an individual could ever ask. The Bible is still as powerful today as it was thousands of years ago. Nothing has changed.

Consider this: every major piece of financial wisdom, from budgeting and saving to investing and giving, can be traced back to Scripture. Much of the advice of thought leaders like Abraham Lincoln, Gandhi, Benjamin Franklin, Roosevelt, Napoleon Hill, and Dale Carnegie is not revolutionary... It's biblical.

A Proven Plan That Stands the Test of Time

The Bible has stood the test of time because its principles are universal and unchanging. Merriam-Webster defines "standing the test of time" as "to continue to be effective, successful, or strong for a long time." Isaiah 40:8 says it even better: "The grass withers, the flower fades, but the word of our God stands forever."

Biblical Money Principles have worked across every era, civilization, and culture—through good times and bad. The lessons taught in Proverbs, Ecclesiastes, and the teachings of Christ are just as relevant today as they were thousands of years ago. Nothing has changed because truth doesn't change.

The Evidence Is Undeniable

If you take the time to research the world's most successful people, you will notice the same trends. Warren Buffett's disciplined investing? It aligns with the biblical principle of stewardship. Henry Ford's emphasis on hard work? It mirrors Proverbs' teachings on diligence. Dale Carnegie's advice on building relationships? It echoes the Bible's guidance on loving others.

Nothing has changed because truth doesn't change.

When I discovered this, it was as if a light bulb had gone off. The secrets to wealth and happiness weren't hidden; they were right in front of me, perfectly structured throughout the pages of Scripture.

Applying the Principles: It's Simple, but Not Easy

As I reflected on everything I had learned, I realized that while the principles themselves are simple, applying them consistently takes discipline. But that's the beauty of biblical wisdom: it doesn't require perfection, just progress.

Here's what I learned:

- **Give generously:** "The righteous give generously." – *Psalm 37:21*
- **Plan, Budget, Spend, and Earn diligently:** "Plans of the diligent lead to profit." – *Proverbs 21:5*
- **Save and Invest consistently:** "Whoever gathers little by little will increase it." – *Proverbs 13:11*
- **Maintain a positive growth mindset:** "As he thinks in his heart, so is he." – *Proverbs 23:7*

These aren't just concepts; they are actionable steps that anyone can take to transform their financial situation and their life.

Success leaves clues, and wisdom stands the test of time. Imagine having the most powerful insights from history's greatest minds and God's Word—all in one place. Proven principles are categorized and ready to guide you toward financial peace and true abundance. Don't just read this book—immerse yourself in the full research of the most impactful quotes and biblical wisdom ever recorded. Take action now—scan the QR code or visit RichbyChoiceBook.com/bibleverses to unlock the knowledge that has transformed lives for generations. Your future self will thank you.

1. Giving: The Heart of Abundance

Giving is not about losing something; it's about gaining a richer life. The Bible repeatedly emphasizes that generosity is a key to living abundantly, a truth echoed by philanthropists and thought leaders throughout history.

Biblical Wisdom:

- *"The righteous give generously."* – Psalm 37:21
- *"Give to others, and you will receive. You will be given much. It will be poured into your hands, more than you can hold."* – Luke 6:38
- *"Whoever gives to the poor will lack nothing."* – Proverbs 28:27
- *"Honor the LORD with your wealth and with the first fruits of all your produce, then your barns will be filled with plenty."* – Proverbs 3:9–10

Timeless Insights:

- *"Giving to those in need will bring more joy than money could ever buy."* – Dave Ramsey
- *"The happiest people are not those getting more, but those giving more."* – Robin Sharma

- *"We make a living by what we get. We make a life by what we give."* – Winston Churchill
- *"For it is in giving that we receive."* – St. Francis of Assisi
- *"Not he who has much is rich, but he who gives much."* – Erich Fromm

John D. Rockefeller, one of the wealthiest men in history, understood this principle. He didn't just give millions away; he started giving 10% of his earnings even when he was making only $1.50 per day. This habit continued throughout his life, leading to his extraordinary generosity.

2. Budgeting, Spending, Earning, and Planning: Master Your Resources

Wealth does not come from how much you make but from how wisely you manage what you have. The Bible provides profound lessons on planning, diligence, and discipline— foundations for financial peace.

Biblical Wisdom:

- *"On the first day of every week, each of you is to put something aside and store it up, as he will prosper."* – 1 Corinthians 16:2
- *"Plans of the diligent lead to wealth."* – Proverbs 21:5
- *"A budget is telling your money where to go instead of wondering where it went."* – Proverbs 29:18
- *"Good planning and hard work lead to prosperity, but hasty shortcuts lead to poverty."* – Proverbs 21:5

Timeless Insights:

- *"You do not save what is left after spending, but spend what is left after saving."* – Warren Buffett
- *"If we command our wealth, we shall be rich and free. If our wealth commands us, we are poor indeed."* – Edmund Burke
- *"Never spend your money before you have it."* – Thomas Jefferson
- *"A goal without a plan is just a wish."* – Antoine de Saint-Exupéry

3. Saving and Investing: Planting Seeds for Tomorrow

Small, consistent savings lead to large rewards over time. Just as a farmer reaps what he sows, those who invest wisely and patiently will see their efforts grow.

Biblical Wisdom:

- *"Whoever gathers little by little will increase it."* – Proverbs 13:11
- *"The wise have wealth and luxury, but fools spend whatever they get."* – Proverbs 21:20
- *"A good person leaves an inheritance for their children's children."* – Proverbs 13:22

Timeless Insights:

- *"The habit of saving is itself an education; it fosters every virtue."* – T.T. Munger

- *"The best investment you can make is in yourself."* – Warren Buffett
- *"Wealth is the ability to fully experience life."* – Henry David Thoreau

4. Positive Growth Mindset: The Engine of Transformation

Your mindset will either be the wind beneath your wings or the weight that holds you down. As the Bible and successful leaders affirm, thoughts shape reality, and faith fuels action.

Biblical Wisdom:

- *"If you believe, you will receive whatever you ask for in prayer."* – Matthew 21:22
- *"Wisdom and understanding are better than having silver and gold."* – Proverbs 16:16
- *"For nothing will be impossible with God."* – Luke 1:37

Timeless Insights:

- *"Whatever the mind of man can conceive and believe, it can achieve."* – Napoleon Hill
- *"Imagination is everything. It is the preview of life's coming attractions."* – Albert Einstein
- *"Do not judge me by my successes; judge me by how many times I fell down and got back up."* – Nelson Mandela

Your financial success starts with a **mindset shift.** Believe in abundance, seek wisdom, and take action with faith. When guided by purpose and discipline, wealth becomes a tool for fulfillment rather than a source of stress.

A Journey Worth Taking

Looking back, my journey started with curiosity but evolved into something much greater. It became a pursuit of truth, not just about money but about life. And the truth I found is this: the Bible is not just a spiritual guide; it's a roadmap for success, wealth, and fulfillment.

In this life, we all live by some sort of compass. Imagine standing at a crossroads, holding a compass that can guide you to incredible destinations. The scary realization, though, is that if we use the wrong compass, chances are that we will arrive at the wrong destination. Without the right compass, you will never get yourself onto the right path, which will never lead to your desired destination.

The Bible, often seen as the greatest guide to life, is also the greatest money book ever written. Ronald Reagan (1984) states, "Within the covers of the Bible are the answers for all the problems men face. In fact, in his Proclamation 5018 on January 25, 1983, President Reagan declared that year as the "Year of the Bible." It offers wisdom on managing resources, giving generously, and planning for the future. When Chelsea and I embraced its teachings and created a financial plan grounded in these fundamentals, everything changed.

The real magic happened for Chelsea and me when we realized the importance of integrating *all* these pillars into our daily lives. For too long, we focused on just a few areas while neglecting others, thinking they weren't as critical. But the truth is that financial peace and prosperity come from mastering the entire framework.

The Fundamentals of Money are like building a house. Each fundamental—giving, budgeting, spending, earning, planning, saving and investing, and having a positive growth mindset—serves as a brick or beam. Neglecting even one piece leaves the structure vulnerable, just as missing beams or bricks can cause a house to crumble. When all parts are in place, your financial house stands strong and secure, able to weather any storm.

Your life will either be by design or default. A life, by default, is a life with the wrong compass, just hopelessly wandering through life. You will never achieve the life you want. But a life by design is a purposeful life. A life of intentional design guided by the right compass will lead you to financial happiness.

When we are aiming to reach the top of the mountain, it is wise to follow the footprints of those who have successfully made the climb before.

It's my hope that by sharing this journey, you, too, will see the incredible power of biblical wisdom. I want you to have an amazing life. Let the Bible be your compass, and watch how it transforms your life. The habits you form today will determine your future. The same principles that built empires and created lasting legacies are available to you. The choice is yours.

What choice will you make? Are you ready to take the first step?

Your Next Step: The Power of a Decision

Now, it's your turn. As you reflect on this, ask yourself:

1. Are you using all of *The Fundamentals of Money* in your daily life, or are you relying only on a few strengths while ignoring the rest?

2. Which of these fundamentals comes naturally to you? Which ones feel like weaknesses that hold you back?

3. What actions can you take today—right now—to turn your financial weaknesses into strengths or automate them to work in your favor?

4. Can you imagine how much peace, freedom, and excitement you'll feel once you begin this journey?

5. If you made a commitment today to fully embrace *The Fundamentals of Money*, how would your life look five years from now? Ten years?

When approached wisely, money is no longer a burden—it becomes an instrument for building a life of purpose, generosity, and abundance.

The truth is, your financial future is in your hands. It's not luck. It's not guesswork. It's a decision.

To explore more faith resources, scan the QR code or visit RichByChoiceBook.com/bibleverses.

Nick and Chelsea Embrace Timeless Wisdom

The Magic Carpet Ride: How Chelsea and I Transformed Our Lives Through The Fundamentals of Money

For years, Chelsea and I were doing well with a few of The Fundamentals of Money, but we weren't fully engaged in all of them. Some came naturally— our strengths that we clung to like a sturdy anchor in shifting tides. Others? They were weaknesses, blind spots we either ignored or simply didn't know how to manage. We thought being strong in a few key areas was enough.

But life has a way of showing you the gaps.

We had dreams, big ones. We wanted peace, security, and abundance—not just financially but in every aspect of our lives. We wanted to give generously, to experience new adventures, and to create a life where we felt fully alive. But to get there, we had to stop treating money as something we just "dealt with" and start seeing it as a powerful tool—one that required mastery.

It was in this realization that everything began to change.

The Turning Point

We made a decision. Instead of operating on autopilot, hoping things would work out, we got intentional. We sat down, looked at our finances, and had the tough conversations. We built on our strengths—using them as our foundation—and found ways to automate our weaknesses so they could no longer trip us up. It wasn't an overnight transformation. But it was a shift—a significant one.

Slowly, we saw things begin to turn. Our cash flow increased. Our net worth multiplied fivefold. More importantly, a sense of peace settled in. The stress around money disappeared. It wasn't about having "more" just for the sake of it—it was about knowing that our money was working for us, not against us. It was about freedom.

And here's the most incredible part: it wasn't just our financial life that changed.

As we applied The Fundamentals of Money with discipline and faith, every part of our lives improved. Our marriage deepened. Our connection with God strengthened. We laughed more, dreamed bigger, and began stepping into the life we once only imagined.

I call it our magic carpet ride, a journey we never would have thought possible. Looking back, I can see the exact moment it started: when we committed to mastering all of The Fundamentals of Money, not by becoming experts overnight but by being intentional and improving just a little every day.

And this is what we want for you.

More peace. More security. More exciting fun and adventure. More love and laughter. A life where money is no longer a source of stress but a powerful tool to create the life of your dreams.

Chelsea and I made that decision years ago, and it changed our lives in ways we never dreamed possible. Now, we invite you to make yours.

Will you take the first step?

PART II

Fundamentals

Three Financial Tales

Ronald James Read was born in Brattleboro, Vermont, and was the first in his family to graduate from high school. After serving in the U.S. military during World War II, he worked as a gas station attendant and janitor for most of his life. Ronald lived humbly, enjoying simple pleasures like a peanut butter English muffin with his coffee each morning and taking an interest in the stock market. When Ronald passed away in 2014 at the age of 92, he made international headlines.

Why? In 2014, nearly 3 million Americans died, but only a small handful—just over 0.1 percent—had a net worth exceeding $8 million. Shockingly, Ronald Read, the janitor, was part of that elite group. He left $2 million to his family, $1.2 million to his local library, and $4.8 million to the hospital where he ate breakfast every morning.

The people who knew Ronald were stunned. How could a janitor have accumulated $8 million? There was no secret life, no lottery win, and no wealthy uncle. Ronald simply saved a little every year, invested in generic blue-chip dividend-paying stocks, and allowed the power of compounding to work its magic.

Remember that last sentence... *let the power of compounding create $8,000,000.00*

Now, meet Richard Fuscone. Richard earned his MBA from the University of Chicago and graduated from Harvard Business School, one of the most prestigious institutions in the world. He rose to the top of Merrill Lynch as executive chairman and president, amassing millions along the way.

Fuscone lived an extravagant lifestyle, taking on enormous amounts of debt to finance it, including a mansion in Armonk, New York, with two swimming pools, six fireplaces, and an indoor space where guests could dine and dance on a see-through covering over the pool.

Just a few years after his retirement, Richard Fuscone filed for bankruptcy. He lost nearly everything. In his bankruptcy documents, he wrote, *"I currently have no income."*

The lesson here isn't that Ronald Read or Richard Fuscone are better or worse people. The point is not that you have to live a simple life to be financially successful or that living extravagantly means certain financial ruin. The difference between these two men was simple: Ronald Read followed the Fundamentals of Money, while Richard Fuscone did not.

Fuscone could have lived a lavish lifestyle without ending up bankrupt. It wasn't the big houses or expensive parties that led to his downfall, but his failure to understand his financial position and the habits required to sustain it. Had Ruscone followed the financial compass I'm about to share with you, he would have been just fine. And the best part? You don't need a Harvard degree to master it.

Let Richard Fuscone's story resonate within you as a reminder that wealth isn't merely about accumulation; it's about understanding, discipline, and making choices aligned with enduring principles. You have the power to write your own narrative, to learn from the highs and lows of others, and to build a foundation that will stand the test of time. The journey to financial success is a road traveled by many, and the map is accessible to all who dare to pursue it.

There are three key takeaways from these stories:

1. Anyone can become wealthy.
2. Anyone can file for bankruptcy.
3. You don't need a fancy degree to achieve financial success.

So, what is the difference between financial success and failure? How do you gain wealth, protect it, and achieve true financial happiness? The answer is simple: *mastering the Fundamentals of Money*. Which you are about to learn. Are you ready?

Six Fundamentals of Money

• Positive Growth Mindset	• Budgeting and Planning
• Giving	• Saving and Investing
• Earning	• Spending

10

Mindset by Choice
Wealth Begins with
How You Think.

Did you know that your brain is composed of around 100 billion neurons? These neurons, like microscopic lightning bolts, constantly transmit and process electrochemical signals. Each second, these neurons fire approximately 200 times. Each neuron is intricately connected to 1,000 others, meaning every time one neuron fires, it shares information with 1,000 more neurons throughout your body. Imagine this: Every single second, your brain sends 20 quadrillion (a million billion) bits of information. This data includes everything from thoughts to the sensation of touch, the colors you see, and the smells you notice—all happening in an instant. The speed and precision of this neural symphony are breathtaking.[47]

20,000,000,000,000,000!

To help visualize the true power of your brain, let's compare it to modern technology. Dr. Robert Reber (2010), Professor of Psychology at Northwestern University, conducted a research study that reveals the brain's ability to process information compared to technology.[48]

- Today's smartphones have gigabytes (16GB, 64 GB, 128 GB, or 1 "Giga" = 1 million; a gigabyte has 1 million characters of information; a smartphone has 16-128 million characters of information).

- The first Apollo Space shuttle that landed on the moon had 64 kilobytes (1 "kilo" = 1 thousand; a kilobyte has 64 thousand characters of information).

- Yahoo, the Internet giant, has created a specially built 2.0-petabyte "data warehouse" (1 petabyte has the equivalent power of about a million gigabytes). Yahoo uses the immense information storage capacity of this data warehouse to analyze the behavior of its half-a-billion monthly visitors. It processes 24 billion events a day. "It is not only the world's single-largest database but also the busiest."[49]

- By comparison, the IRS's own massive data warehouse, which keeps track of 300-plus million Americans and many more businesses, has a capacity of 150 terabytes of memory. Yet Yahoo's 2.0-petabyte computational center, which can process 24 billion "events" a day, is a full 20 percent smaller than the capacity of a single human brain.

- The human brain's memory storage capacity is something closer to around 2.5 petabytes (1 petabyte has the equivalent power of about a million gigabytes). For comparison, if your brain worked like a digital video recorder in a television, 2.5 petabytes, which is comparable to the power of your brain, would be enough to hold three million hours of TV shows. You would have to leave the TV running continuously for more than 300 years to use up all that storage.

Your brain's potential is limitless and extraordinary. As Jim Kwik, a leading expert in brain performance, said, "Our most precious gift is our brain.

The human brain is 20 percent more powerful than Yahoo's largest data warehouse.

If our mindset is not aligned with our desires or goals, we will never achieve them."[50] The true power of the human brain remains largely untapped, and we've barely scratched the surface of its capabilities.

Think of it as your very own "Super-Computer," a marvel of nature designed to process, create, and accomplish astonishing feats when harnessed properly. Understanding this is the first step to unlocking its full potential.

The Conscious and Unconscious Brain

Imagine a swimmer gliding effortlessly across a vast ocean. This swimmer is your conscious brain, fully in control of every stroke, aware of the direction, and feeling the cool touch of the water. Every ripple, every sound of the waves crashing, is a deliberate choice. This is your conscious mind, making decisions, focusing on tasks, and engaging with the world in real time. But beneath that swimmer lies the immense, mysterious expanse of the ocean—your unconscious brain—as deep and powerful as the sea itself, silently working in the background.

To truly grasp the power of your unconscious mind, consider the ocean. Covering more than 70 percent of the Earth's surface and holding 1.332 billion cubic kilometers of water, the ocean is a force of nature. Within its depths, some parts reach nearly 36,000 feet, such as the Mariana Trench—so deep that if Mount Everest were submerged, its peak would still be over a mile underwater. The ocean holds about 352 quintillion gallons of water, with powerful currents flowing beneath the surface, moving like invisible rivers that shape weather patterns and support marine life.

Your unconscious mind is like these ocean currents—vast, constant, and incredibly powerful. Just as these currents drive the ocean's movement without ever being seen, your unconscious brain guides countless daily functions: regulating your heartbeat, digesting food, processing emotions, and even controlling your breathing, all without you having to think about it. Like the ocean, it operates with such quiet strength that you're often unaware of its influence. Research suggests that 95–99 percent of our brain activity occurs unconsciously, beneath the surface of our awareness.[51] [52]

As the swimmer moves across the water, they may believe they are in control, but the truth is that the ocean's currents are guiding much of their journey. The unconscious mind directs your habits, instincts, and reactions, much like the powerful Gulf Stream current, which moves nearly 150 times faster than the Amazon River, shaping entire ecosystems and influencing global weather. Think about how walking, once a conscious effort as a child, is now second nature, driven by the unconscious brain. You can walk, talk, and plan your day simultaneously without thinking about the mechanics of each step.

With its vast, uncharted depths and relentless currents, the ocean is a powerful metaphor for your mind. Though your conscious mind may control immediate actions, it is a swimmer in the vast and powerful sea of subconscious activity, where most of your brain's work occurs beyond your awareness. Understanding this can open the door to a new appreciation for just how powerful your mind truly is.

You hold the ultimate power over your mind and its focus. No barrier can hold you back when you guide your mind with purpose. How exciting is this? Can you imagine the possibilities? James Allen said, "You are today where your thoughts have brought you; you will be tomorrow where your thoughts take you."[53] Your thoughts are the architects of your reality, and where you choose to direct them shapes your life. But the question is: How can you harness this incredible power to achieve the life you desire?

The answer is simple and easy. Your mind is a powerful tool. When you fill it with positive thoughts, your life will begin to change. Here are three ways you can start enhancing the power of your mind right now. At the end of the chapter, I will give you an easy daily exercise that I use that encompasses all three powers.

1. Neuroplasticity
2. Cognitive Behavior Therapy
3. Gratitude

Neuroplasticity: The Power to Rewire Your Brain

Neuroplasticity is nothing short of a miracle of the human brain—the ability to change, adapt, and grow by forming new neural pathways and circuits. Every thought, every experience, and every challenge you embrace rewires your brain to function in a way that aligns with the life you want. Think of it as training your mind to become a powerful tool that works in your favor rather than against you.

"When you rule your mind, you rule your world."[54] This quote resonates even deeper when you understand neuroplasticity. It means your mind can be shaped and molded to create the reality you desire. James Allen beautifully said, "As he thinks, so he is; as he continues to think, so he remains."[55] Your beliefs and thoughts form the foundation of your reality.

This truth is echoed by Henry Ford: "Whether you think you can, or you think you can't, you're right."[56] The brain's plasticity means that it can support whichever thought pattern you nurture. Focus on growth, success, and abundance; your brain will pave the way for it to manifest in your life. You can shape your future by training your brain to focus on positive outcomes.

- ~~I will never be happy.~~ I can and will be happy.
- ~~My entire family has always been stressed and poor.~~ I can change my family's life for the better forever.

Cognitive Behavior Therapy: Master Your Mindset

Cognitive Behavior Therapy (CBT) is a powerful tool for mastering how your thoughts influence your feelings and actions. It's based on a simple yet profound idea: Your thoughts create your world. What you think directly affects how you feel; those feelings shape your actions and, ultimately, your reality. As Earl Nightingale wisely stated, "Whatever we plant in our subconscious mind and nourish with repetition and emotion will one day become a reality."[57]

The question becomes, *how* do we guide our subconscious mind to work toward the life we desire? The answer lies in what you believe and tell yourself. James Allen said, "As he thinks, so he is; as he continues to think, so he remains."[58] What you think drives how you feel, which then determines your actions and future.

In Proverbs 23:7, the Bible reinforces this truth: "For as he thinks in his heart, so is he." This isn't just about what you consciously think but about the deeper beliefs you hold in your core or, as the Bible calls it, your heart. This inner process of thoughts and emotions works together to define your actions and outcomes.

Albert Einstein once said, "Imagination is everything. It is the preview of life's coming attractions."[59] What you consistently imagine and believe has the power to become your reality. After studying the most successful people of his time, the legendary Napoleon Hill concluded, "Both poverty and riches are the offspring of thought."[60] The thoughts you hold about money, success, and happiness will shape your financial reality.

The key to financial success and happiness and becoming Rich by Choice lies in a mindset that believes you can achieve it. Andrew Carnegie, one of the wealthiest men in history, summed it up perfectly: "I took possession of my own mind, and that mind has yielded me every material thing I want and much more than I need."[61] It's not about luck; it's about harnessing the power of your mind to believe in and work toward the life you desire.

Gratitude: The Secret to Abundance

Gratitude is perhaps the simplest yet most profound way to shift your mindset and unlock a life of abundance. As

Plato said, "A grateful mind is a great mind which eventually attracts itself great things."[62] When you focus on what you already have, you invite more of it into your life. Gratitude rewires your brain to see abundance rather than lack, which is the first step toward creating even more wealth, happiness, and success.

John Templeton, a legendary philanthropist and investor, believed that "An attitude of gratitude creates blessings."[63] The act of being grateful not only enriches your current life but also opens the door to greater possibilities. When you express gratitude, you send a powerful signal to the universe—and your brain—that you are ready to receive even more.

Gratitude is more than a response to what's going well in your life; it's an active practice that shifts your focus toward abundance. When you are a good steward of the blessings you already have, more will flow into your life. As you grow in gratitude, your mindset will align with the limitless potential of life, and opportunities for growth, wealth, and joy will follow.

Harness the Power of Your Mind: Nick's Happy Habits

Your mind is your greatest asset. It has the power to shape your reality, determine your success, and unlock a life of true abundance. The thoughts you choose, the habits you cultivate, and the words you speak over yourself all contribute to the life you are building.

If you want to experience more joy, wealth, and fulfillment, you must first train your mind to seek it. Gratitude, intention, and faith are the cornerstones of a mindset that attracts opportunity, and when practiced consistently, they transform not just your finances but your entire life.

That's why I've created Nick's Happy Habits. A simple yet powerful set of daily practices designed to rewire your mind for success, gratitude, and abundance. These habits will help you focus on what truly matters, strengthen your faith, and bring more joy into your life.

Start today because your future is waiting, and it begins with the choices you make right now.

1. **Morning Gratitude**: Each morning, write down three things you are grateful for. Even on tough days, focus on what you *could* be grateful for. This habit trains your mind to seek joy, and over time, your life will be filled with a sense of abundance. As Sir John Templeton believed, *"When I am grateful, I am rich."*

2. **Three-Minute Journal**: Spend three minutes journaling about a happy event from the past day. Use emotional language to describe how it made you feel. This will help you relive the joy and deepen your gratitude for the small moments that make life beautiful.

3. **Compliment with Intention**: Give a heartfelt compliment to someone you care about. Meaningful connections create richer, happier relationships, and this simple act of kindness strengthens bonds and brings more love into your life.

4. **Daily Meditation**: Daily meditation is a powerful practice that allows you to quiet the mind, focus your thoughts, and visualize the life you desire. To meditate on Financial Happiness, close your eyes and imagine yourself living in abundance, feeling wealthy, happy, and secure. See yourself applying the Fundamentals of Money effortlessly, surrounded by

loving relationships, great health, and the life you've always dreamed of, knowing that each moment of meditation brings you closer to that reality. Feel excited and all the wonderful emotions as if you have already achieved your goals.

5. **Daily Affirmations from Scripture**: Read aloud these paraphrased Bible verses each morning and night to align your heart and mind with abundance and faith:

   ○ "Riches, wealth, and happiness are gifts from God. He wants me to enjoy the abundance He provides" (Ecclesiastes 5:19).
   ○ "God grants me my heart's desires and fulfills my purpose" (Psalm 20:4).
   ○ "God takes pleasure in my prosperity and loves blessing me" (Psalm 35:27).

● ● ●

The human mind is one of the most powerful tools you possess. A positive growth mindset is a very important Fundamental of Money. It is essential for financial success. To achieve Financial Happiness, you must first empower your mind. Remember, understanding leads to achievement, and belief fuels that achievement. What you think, you become.

I want you to think back to the "Life You Want" exercise you performed in Chapter 7: Design by Choice. That vision wasn't just a dream; it was a preview of what's possible. Every single day, remind yourself: *I can have that life. I will have the life of my dreams.* See yourself waking up in the home you envisioned, surrounded by love, laughter, and limitless possibilities. Feel the joy, the excitement, and the deep fulfillment of knowing you built this life by design, not by default. The more vividly you visualize it, the more real it becomes—because the life you desire is not just within reach; it's already unfolding before you.

By embracing neuroplasticity, mastering your thoughts through CBT, and practicing gratitude, you can reshape your mind to support your goals and dreams. Financial Happiness and being Rich by Choice are not just a destination—they're a mindset. Take control of your thoughts today, and watch as your life transforms into the abundant, joyful, and financially free existence you deserve. The time is now—embrace the power of your mind and let it guide you toward being Rich by Choice.

To explore resources from this book, scan the QR code or visit RichByChoiceBook.com/bonus.

Nick and Chelsea's Awareness Habits

One of the ways I remain aware is by actively questioning myself. Here is a list of sample questions.

- If someone followed you and observed your inner dialogue about money, what would they hear most: confidence and optimism or doubt and worry? Are your thoughts helping you build the life you want, or are they subtly holding you back?

- When you imagine your ideal future, do you think of it as something you can create through daily actions, or do you believe external circumstances determine your success? How often do you take ownership of your financial and personal outcomes, and where can you take more control?

- Do you view your current financial situation as a fixed reality, or do you believe that even small daily improvements can transform your future over time? How can you start shifting your focus from what you lack today to what you can create tomorrow?

- Do you believe you can and deserve to be happy? Do you believe you have the choice to be happy?

- Do you believe you have the power to choose to be happy and successful, are within your control, influenced by your daily thoughts and habits? If not, what stories are you telling yourself that prevent you from embracing a mindset of abundance and growth?

Join me in growing your awareness on your path to becoming Rich by Choice.

11

Growth by Choice
The Secret of Success Is
Knowing How to Save, Earn,
Spend, and Give.

It Adds Up

Many years ago, a spirited Texan named Cindy walked into my office. With her thick accent, boots, and jeans, she radiated warmth and energy. Yet, despite her vibrant personality, Cindy was convinced she could never be wealthy. "Investing," she said, "is for rich people. I barely make it to payday each month."

Smiling, I gently agreed, acknowledging her frustration. But I asked, "Since you're already here, would you be open to a quick exercise to see if there's a way we can improve things?" Reluctantly, she agreed.

It was mid-afternoon, and I reached for a pen and note-pad. "Cindy, walk me through your day so far," I asked. As we retraced her steps, a pattern emerged:

- Morning Starbucks coffee: $7
- Bagel and Dr. Pepper with a friend at the office: $9
- Mid-morning vape and snack: $7
- Lunch out: $15
- Afternoon Starbucks run: $7
- Happy Hour plans with friends: $30
- Gas for her truck to drive between all these spots: $10

By the end, we tallied her daily spending: $85. (This didn't even include her eight monthly subscriptions, three of which she never uses.) I smiled and asked, "Cindy, if I could show you a way to become a millionaire without making drastic life changes, would you be interested?"

Her eyes widened. "Of course!"

I explained, "Let's say you give up just one of these expenses, maybe that $7 Starbucks coffee in the afternoon. That's $7 a day, $210 a month, and $2,520 a year. If you invest that at a 14 percent return in 10 years, you could have over $50,000. In 20 years, close to $300,000. In 30 years, that's almost $1,200,000. And in 40 years? Almost $5,000,000."

Cindy was astonished. "Just $7 a day?" she asked, disbe-lief turning into excitement.

"Yes," I said. "Small changes lead to big wealth." It worked for Cindy, and it can work for you too. Can you imagine the wealth you could build with multiple small changes? Sometimes, all it takes is one simple shift to turn your financial dreams into reality.

Becoming a multimillionaire doesn't require a genius IQ, a six-figure salary, or a lucky break—just small, consistent choices made daily. The following four graphs prove that simple tweaks in your everyday spending can unlock a future of abundance. These charts aren't just numbers—they're your roadmap to wealth, peace, and financial freedom.

Saving $7/Day

Just $7 a day = $210 a month = $2,555 a year

Investing $7/Day

→ 10 years = $55,737.54
→ 20 years = $281,703.73
→ 30 years = $1,197,795.90
→ 40 years = $4,911,732.78

Saving $15/Day

Just $15 a day = $450 a month = $5,475 a year

Investing $15/Day

→ 10 years = $119,437.58
→ 20 years = $603,650.85
→ 30 years = $2,566,705.49
→ 40 years = $10,525,148.09

Saving $25/Day

Just $25 a day = $750 a month = $9,125 a year

Investing $25/Day

→ 10 years = $199,062.63
→ 20 years = $1,006,084.75
→ 30 years = $4,277,842.49
→ 40 years = $17,541,913.49

Saving $50/Day

Just $50 a day = $1,500 a month = $18,250 a year

Investing $50/Day

→ 10 years = $398,125.26
→ 20 years = $2,012,169.50
→ 30 years = $8,555,684.98
→ 40 years = $35,083,826.98

Wealth isn't out of reach. It's possible for anyone willing to make small, consistent changes. How powerful is that? One simple decision, one daily habit, can set you on a path to financial success. What's more exciting than knowing that *you* have the power to create this kind of wealth?

A journey of a thousand miles begins with a single step.

—Lao Tzu

What if your journey to becoming a multimillionaire began today with just $7? The secret isn't in massive, overwhelming changes. It's in those small, consistent actions that build momentum over time.

Cindy didn't become a millionaire overnight; it resulted from tiny, deliberate choices compounded by time and discipline. Your journey can start the same way. It doesn't take extraordinary wealth or massive sacrifice; it starts with one change and a commitment to a better future.

So, how did Cindy know what changes to make? Where did her path to millions begin? It all started with a budget—a simple plan to manage her money, direct her actions, and create her wealth. And now, you have that same opportunity to harness the power of small daily actions to create the future you've always dreamed of and become Rich by Choice.

The Every-Penny Budget: Saving and Spending Responsibly

Many people cringe when they hear the word "budget," seeing it as restrictive or dull, but in reality, it's one of the most liberating tools you can have on your journey to Financial Happiness. Think of it as the fuel for your car on your financial road trip. How far can you go without knowing how much gas you have?

You have to know where your money is going. The Every-Penny budget lets you see exactly where your money goes, giving you the insights needed to make necessary changes. It shows you where to find that extra $7 a day, the same $7 that could turn into millions over time.

Here's the beauty of it: an Every-Penny budget works for everyone. Whether you're struggling financially, comfortably in the middle, or living in luxury, tracking your spending is the key to making smarter choices. If you're living paycheck to paycheck, your budget will reveal where small changes can make a big difference. If you're wealthy, your budget can show where your resources are underutilized, helping you make your money work harder. No matter your income level, everyone benefits from an Every-Penny budget.

So, how do you create this game-changing tool? It's simple. Track every penny you spend for a month—big or

No matter your income level, everyone benefits from an Every-Penny budget.

small, it all counts. If writing everything down seems over-whelming, many ways exist to simplify the process. Many banks and credit unions offer budgeting tools that automatically categorize your spending if you primarily use your debit or credit card. Alternatively, numerous budgeting apps are available, making it easier than ever to log and analyze every dollar you spend. What matters most is that *you do it*. Find what works best for you and commit.

Creating an Every-Penny budget is your first step toward unlocking the power of your finances and becoming Rich by Choice. With just a small shift in awareness, you'll be empowered to reach your full potential and make meaningful changes that can lead to a wealthier, happier life.

Budget Musts

You've worked hard for your money: long hours, mental fatigue, and dealing with challenges day in and day out. Over 40 hours a week, 52 weeks a year, that's 2080 hours of hard work. In a lifetime, the average person spends about 90,000 hours working. If you're dedicating that much of your life to earning money, doesn't it make sense to spend just a few minutes creating a budget to make sure your hard work pays off?

Whether you use a pen and paper, an Excel spreadsheet, or budgeting software, the method doesn't matter; what matters is *doing it*. Write down all your income and expenses. Get a clear view of where your money is going, and don't spend more than you make. That's the most basic yet crucial rule for building a solid financial future. If you consistently spend more than you earn, no one can help fix that.

A budget gives you the clarity to decide what you spend your money on. It shows you exactly where your money is going so you can take control of your finances and prioritize what truly matters to you.

As you review your budget, ask yourself:

- Does this bring me joy?
- Is this more important than financial security in the future?
- Can I find a less expensive option?
- How often do I use this?
- Is this essential or just a nice-to-have?
- Is this more important than getting to live the future life I designed in Chapter 7: Design by Choice?
- Is this bringing more joy than the life I have always dreamed of?

Ask yourself honestly: Is this purchase bringing me more happiness now than being financially free in the future?

This is your money, your life. You know what makes you happy. The beauty of this strategy is that you don't have to change your lifestyle drastically. You can build wealth and secure your financial future by making small, intentional adjustments.

Our goal is simple: use this strategy for every small change, and you are that much closer to enjoying a life of being Rich by Choice.

Exercise: Calculating Savings Rate

Let me tell you a story about my dear friends, John and Stephanie. They're two of the kindest, sweetest, most grounded people you'll ever meet: John, a pastor with a passion for motorcycles. I call him "The Motorcycle Pastor." Stephanie is a dedicated teacher. They have lived a life full of meaning and purpose. Every summer, they embark on a cross-country motorcycle trip, exploring the beauty of the US. Can you imagine other bikers' expressions when they learn John is a pastor? Their journey to being Rich by Choice didn't start in a place of abundance. In fact, when they were younger, they were barely making ends meet, living paycheck to paycheck with little room to save.

The powerful part is that despite their tight finances, they committed to saving just 1 percent of their monthly income. That's it. Just 1 percent. It might not sound like much, but the key is that they got started. That first small step was the spark that ignited their path to financial success. Slowly but surely, as they gained more stability, they increased their savings rate: first to 2 percent, then 3 percent, and as they received raises and promotions, they pushed it to 4 percent.

Today, John and Stephanie are living the dream. They've become millionaires, retired, financially free, and enjoying life to the fullest. They travel the country on their motorcycles, savoring every moment, all because they decided to start saving, even when it seemed like a small drop in the vast ocean.

Once you create your budget, you'll be able to see your own savings rate, which is simply the percentage of your gross annual income that you save. It's easy math. Let's say you earn $100,000 a year and save $1,000 a month, or $12,000 a year. Divide $12,000 by your $100,000 income, and voila, your savings rate is 12 percent. It's that simple difference between what you make and what you spend.

Start small, just like John and Stephanie did. The power lies in getting started, no matter how modest the amount. Over time, as you commit to saving, your wealth will grow—little by little, drop by drop—until one day, you'll look back and realize you've built something truly remarkable.

Here's how you can calculate your savings rate, which is simply the percentage of your gross annual income that you save.

Formula:

Savings Rate = (Annual Savings/Gross Annual Income) x 100

Let's assume your gross annual income is $100,000, and you save $1,000 per month, which totals $12,000 per year.

Example 1: Yearly

Savings Rate = (12,000/100,000) x 100
Savings Rate = 12 percent

Example 2: Monthly

You save $1,000 per month, and there are 12 months in a year:

Savings Rate = ((1,000 x 12)/100,000) x 100
Savings Rate = 12 percent

Each method gives you the same result, showing you the percentage of your income you're saving. Understanding this number is a crucial beginning step in taking control of your finances and working toward your financial goals. But you must get started.

Meet Linda

Linda's story is one of resilience and triumph. She was a single mom who struggled her entire life to make ends meet. Month after month, it was a battle just to keep the lights on and food on the table. But if you ask Linda about those years, she'll tell you she has no regrets – her kids grew up happy, healthy, and successful, which was always her greatest goal.

But when the last of her children moved out, something remarkable happened. Linda was 50 years old and suddenly found herself with extra breathing room in her budget. I call this her "Empty Nest Pay Raise." For the first time, she had a little extra income to enjoy life, but she made a smart decision: She also invested a portion of it toward her future. Linda, who had struggled for so long, began saving 15 percent of her $75,000 salary each year, investing it wisely at a 14 percent annual return.

By the time she retired at 70, Linda had saved over $1,000,000! She started at 50 years old with no previous savings, and yet she still achieved financial freedom. What brings Linda the most joy isn't the number in her bank account; it's the freedom she has now. After years of scraping by, she now lives her life with a deep sense of security and happiness that she never thought possible. Every time I see Linda, she has a radiant smile on her face. She's experiencing financial happiness in ways she never dreamed of, and so can you.

You have the power to control your savings rate, and no matter where you are right now, it's never too late to start. Even if you can't save 10 percent yet, that's okay. Even if you begin by saving *just 1 percent,* you can increase it as your situation improves. Think of John and Stephanie, the motorcycle pastor and his wife. They started small, too, and now they spend all their days traveling and enjoying the life they want. If you want to save more, earning more can help.

Earning by Choice: Unlocking Your Full Potential

Get ready for a fun challenge—it's time to play *Guess Who I Am!* I'll give you clues, and your job is to figure out who I'm describing. Let's see if you can guess before the final hint!

Because his home life was "chaotic" and "abusive," he left home when he was 17. He later worked as a janitor and did not attend college. One day, he asked his landlord how he became successful; he told him to attend a Jim Rohn seminar. "I made the big decision to spend a week's pay to go to this event, and I sat there and was mesmerized. I was taught to work harder on myself. And that's what started the game for me." This is Tony Robbins, *New York Times* #1 best-selling author and billionaire.

• • •

A single mom struggling with depression and trying to survive on welfare. Her parents said she had an amusing, overactive imagination. She aspired to be an author, but her manuscript received tons of rejections, one after another. Filled with perseverance, she kept working harder, learning, writing, and improving. Her first book turned into a series that sold over 500 million copies in over 200 territories. It has been translated into 80 languages and turned into eight blockbuster films and spin-offs. This is JK Rowling, creator and author of Harry Potter. Rowling was the first author to be included on the Forbes Billionaires list but lost her billionaire status after donating a big portion of her fortune.

• • •

As a young lawyer and inspiring politician in Springfield, Illinois, he failed in business and politics for many years. Failure after failure. He would publicly attack and ridicule his opponents. Even publishing ugly letters in newspapers. One day, he went too far and was too hateful and ugly. His opponent, filled with rage, challenged him to a duel. A fight to the death. Choosing swords as their weapons of choice, both men showed up at dawn, just as the sun began to break, on a sandbar in the Mississippi River. Both were prepared to fight to the death. By the grace of God, at the very last second, his second-in-command interrupted and stopped the duel. This man learned a valuable lesson. From that point on, he learned to be calm, collected, and in control of his emotions. He worked hard to never criticize anyone again. This is Abraham Lincoln, the 16th U.S. President from 1861–1865, ranked as history's highest-ranked and favorite US President.

• • •

Success isn't reserved for the privileged or the lucky—it's built through perseverance, grit, and relentless self-improvement. Your ability to earn and create wealth is directly tied to your willingness to grow. If you want more in life, you must become more. The greatest investment[IP] you can make is in yourself—your knowledge, your skills, and your mindset.

You don't need a prestigious degree to succeed. You need relentless learning and a willingness to grow. Warren Buffett, one of the richest men alive, was terrified of public speaking.

So he spent $100 on a Dale Carnegie course—a tiny investment that led to billions in value. To this day, he keeps that certificate displayed more prominently than his Columbia degree. Small choices, when made consistently, create massive results.

Your Greatest Investment Ever^{IP}: How to Invest in Yourself

Your Greatest Investment Ever is the powerhouse within you: your skills, mindset, habits, and capacity to grow—the part of your financial plan that compounds faster than the stock market when nurtured with intention. This framework teaches you how to strategically invest in yourself to multiply your value in the marketplace and your impact in the world. When you fuel your income engine, you don't just earn more; you become more. The greatest asset you'll ever invest in is you.

Small choices, when made consistently, create massive results.

The Growth Grid^{IP}

The Growth Grid is a personal elevation system designed to help you expand who you are, not just what you earn. It's built on essential habits that strengthen your mind, skills, relationships, purpose, and peace. Whether reading, refining your craft, seeking mentors, or surrounding yourself with growth-minded people, every category on this grid fuels your long-term success. It's a simple truth: When you grow, everything around you grows. This is how you become invaluable in business, unstoppable in life, and unshakable in purpose.

The Growth Grid Categories

To maximize its impact for your benefit, use a journal or digital tracker to rate yourself weekly in each category, reflect on wins or setbacks, and set one small, bold goal for growth in each category. You do not have to conquer the world in one day. Great success is achieved by small, consistent actions.

- **Feed Your Mind:** Read books that challenge and inspire you. Ten pages a day could change your entire trajectory.

- **Sharpen Your Skills:** Become invaluable by consistently improving your craft.

- **Find Mentors:** Learn from those who've already climbed the mountain you want to reach.

- **Take Action:** Knowledge without execution is useless. Apply what you learn immediately.

- **Surround Yourself with Growth-Minded People:** Your environment shapes your future. Choose wisely.

- **Attend seminars and workshops.** There's always something new to learn.

- **Grow your heart.** Be more caring, loving, and compassionate. The world needs more of that.

- **Develop mindfulness.** A daily meditation practice can sharpen your focus and calm your mind.

- **Find joy in your work.** The more you love what you do, the better you'll become.

- **Build connections.** Nurture your social and business networks—they're invaluable resources.
- **Keep learning.** Whether it's through formal education or life experiences, never stop.

We have created a simple, ready-to-use Growth Grid for you. You can access it by scanning the QR code at the end of the chapter.

Consider Dr. Seuss. Twenty-seven publishers rejected his first book. Let that sink in—twenty-seven closed doors. But he didn't give up. The twenty-eighth publisher took a chance on him, and that book went on to sell six million copies. He became one of the most beloved authors in history, with over 100 million copies sold. What if he had stopped at the twenty-seventh rejection? His story is a testament to perseverance, belief in oneself, and the power of improvement. I want you to be able to maximize your earnings potential.

Spending by Choice: Have Fun

When I was young,
I was always jealous,
Always yearning to be bigger, to be older,
Chasing the future with impatient hands,
Reaching for more, craving the next step.
My siblings, they were my giants,
Driving through the night, laughing with friends,
And I, just dying to join them,
Dying to be in high school, to taste that freedom.
But when I got there, it wasn't enough.

Their college lives sparkled brighter—
Moving out, staying late, eating pizza at midnight.
And I, dying once more,
Dying to leave high school behind,
Chasing the thrill of independence.

Yet, when college came,
I found myself watching them again—
They were working, making money,
And I had none.
I was dying to graduate,
Dying to step into the world of work and wealth.

But then the world of work came,
And with it, the weight of responsibility,
The endless hours, the stress,
And I, again, was dying—
Dying for retirement,
For the promise of peace and rest.

Now, here I am.
Sixty-five, dying of something deeper,
Dying of cancer.
And with this final chapter,
I look back and see a life lived for what was next,
Not for what was now.

I regret the days I didn't savor,
The sunsets missed while looking ahead,
The laughter I let slip by,
The joy I traded for the illusion of greener grass.

Now, as I fade,
I wish I had stopped dying to live,
And simply lived.

My time is up, but you still have time,
So live with a passion, bold and sublime.
Laugh, love, and live—let your spirit soar high,
For life is too fleeting to just let pass by.

—Anonymous Author

Living for Today While Preparing for Tomorrow

Life isn't meant to be lived in a constant chase for "what's next." Too often, we postpone joy—waiting for the perfect moment, the perfect income, the perfect circumstances—only to realize too late that life has passed us by. Financial happiness isn't about extremes. It's about balance—learning to spend wisely while still embracing the beauty of the present.

Some of my most treasured memories didn't come from extravagant spending but from intentional experiences. Like the time my little princess Kinsley, barely able to reach the gas pedal, beat me in a go-kart race—her victory grin worth more than any possession. Or when Daegen, my son, took me out in a "Fathers vs Sons" paintball match. Leaving me **Money is a tool, not a goal.** with a bruised ego and an even bigger bruise on my backside. These moments didn't drain a bank account, but they filled my soul.

Money is a tool, not a goal. The goal isn't to hoard it out of fear or recklessly spend it without a plan. It's to use it in a way that aligns with what truly matters—memories, relationships, security, and freedom.

The Art of Intentional Spending

- **Spend on experiences, not just things.** The best returns on investment often come in the form of laughter, adventure, and time well spent.
- **Live with purpose.** Know where your money is going, and make sure it aligns with what truly brings you happiness.
- **Balance joy and responsibility.** Prepare for the future, but don't let it rob you of the present.

Giving by Choice: The Power

I once knew a pastor who had an undeniable passion for motorcycles. This wasn't the "motorcycle pastor" who rides across the country—no, this was a man who loved the art of fixing up bikes, the hum of an engine roaring to life under his hands. His workshop was his sanctuary, filled with tools and dreams. But one day, his wife came to him and said with a laugh, "You've got to stop giving away motorcycles!"

At first, it sounds puzzling, doesn't it? How could their garage be overflowing if he kept *giving* motorcycles away? The truth is, every time he gave from the heart, something miraculous happened. He would fix up a bike, gift it to someone in need, and in return, he would randomly receive another motorcycle. And they were newer, nicer, even more expensive motorcycles. Before he knew it, their garage was bursting at the seams with gifts from others.

This pastor and his wife understood something profound: *The Power of Giving*. It's a universal truth as ancient as time itself—when you give with a heart full of joy and love, you receive far more than you could ever imagine. And it's not just about the material things. The more you give, the more you open your life to abundance—whether in kindness, opportunities, or blessings.

"The best way to find yourself is to lose yourself in the service of others," said Gandhi. This pastor didn't give motorcycles because he felt he had to; he gave because he *wanted* to. His heart was alive with the joy of helping others, and in return, the blessings multiplied. The intention behind the act is where the real magic lies. When you give freely, without strings attached, from a place of genuine happiness, that energy comes back to you in ways you can't even begin to predict.

I've seen this truth unfold time and again. Clients, friends, and mentors all tell me the same thing: *The moment they began giving consistently, their wealth—and their lives— began to flourish.*

When you give, you set in motion a powerful law of attraction. What you send out, you will receive. It's inevitable. Every time you give, you will be drawn closer to the abundance life offers. The more you give, the more you'll receive in return, and your faith in this beautiful law of life will grow stronger each day.

Research has shown that those who give consistently live happier, healthier, and wealthier lives. So, whatever you have to give—your money, your time, your love—*give it*. Winston Churchill once said, *"We make a living by what we get, but we make a life by what we give."* Give freely, give joyfully, and watch as the world returns your gifts, multiplied many times over. The life you've always dreamed of is just on the other side of giving.

Imagine a life where financial stress no longer dictates your choices. Where each dollar spent brings joy rather than regret, and every penny saved is a seed planted for a brighter tomorrow. By mastering the art of budgeting, you've harnessed the power to transform spending into joyful, intentional decisions that nurture your dreams and relationships.

By embracing your true potential, you've turned earning into an empowering journey of continual growth, purpose, and abundance. And through the generous act of giving, you've unlocked the profound joy of creating lasting impact, experiencing how generosity not only enriches others but multiplies blessings back into your own life.

This isn't theory—it's your reality waiting to happen. Commit today to budgeting wisely, spending intentionally, earning passionately, and giving joyfully. The extraordinary life you've envisioned—rich in peace, overflowing with fulfillment, and radiant with happiness—is not only possible, it's yours to claim. Choose this path and step forward confidently, knowing you're truly becoming Rich by Choice.

To explore resources from this book, scan the QR code or visit RichByChoiceBook.com/bonus.

Nick and Chelsea's Growth Inspiration

Do you remember my mom? My hero. A single mom of four boys, juggling three jobs to keep the lights on. Her life was filled with storms—relentless waves of struggle and hardship crashing down on her. But she didn't just stand there waiting for the clouds to part. She took action.

One day, I asked her how she managed to push through. She looked at me and said, "Nick, every month, no matter how tight things got, I did whatever it took to put $10 in a white envelope and never touched it."

That small act was monumental for her. A $10 bill may seem insignificant to some, but for her, it was a sacrifice. And yet, it brought her something priceless: joy and peace. Imagine that. While everything around her was chaos, that simple act of saving gave her hope.

It wasn't just about the money. It was about taking control, even in a world that felt uncontrollable. "Before I knew it," she said, "I was able to put away $20, then $100." What began as a small, almost invisible step became a path to a brighter future.

Today, by the grace of God and her unwavering perseverance, my mother lives a life she once only dreamed of. She's financially free, traveling whenever and wherever she pleases. She spends time with her grandchildren, making memories on her own terms and living with the happiness she had once only envisioned.

The power of saving isn't in the amount; it's in the act of starting. Take that first step, however small, and watch how the journey unfolds. What matters is that you start. My own mother began saving $10 a month.

And guess what? She's a millionaire today. Your dream of financial happiness isn't out of reach. Just start, like my mother did, and soon, you'll realize the peace and freedom that comes with it. Her story is proof that small beginnings can lead to extraordinary outcomes, and so can yours.

12

Debt by Choice
Another Secret of Success:
When to Make Debt Work for You.

There's a timeless story about an English professor who walked into class one day and wrote a seemingly simple sentence on the board:

A WOMAN WITHOUT HER MAN IS NOTHING

She called two students to the front—one man, one woman—and handed each of them a marker. Their task? To punctuate the sentence.

The young man confidently stepped forward first. In a matter of seconds, he turned the phrase into:

A WOMAN WITHOUT HER MAN, IS NOTHING.

He stood back, satisfied with his interpretation. Then, the young woman approached the board, shook her head with a knowing smile, and made her own adjustments:

A WOMAN: WITHOUT HER, MAN IS NOTHING.

In that moment, the whole class saw the power of perspective. Two people looked at the same sentence, yet what they saw—what they understood—was vastly different. This story offers a profound lesson: A small shift in perspective can change everything.

> *When you change the way you look at things,*
> *the things you look at change.*
> —Wayne Dyer

The same is true when it comes to money. For instance, consider the concept of interest: some people earn interest on their savings, while others pay it. Two sides of the same coin, yet the experience is worlds apart. A simple change in perspective can define a life of financial growth or perpetual debt.

According to the *Wall Street Journal* and National Payroll Week, 70 percent of Americans live paycheck to paycheck.[64] Take a moment to think about that: 7 out of 10 people in your life are just barely getting by. And the most surprising part? You might not even know it. Why? Because many are caught in a cycle of overspending and accumulating debt. We live in a culture obsessed with winning an invisible competition: collecting more things and spending more money to impress people who likely don't matter. It's a chase that leads to nowhere.

*Too many people spend money they haven't earned to buy
things they don't want, to impress people they don't like.*

—Will Rogers

It's a trap, and many of us have fallen into it at one point
or another. Yet, the happiness we seek through material
goods is fleeting, a mirage that fades the closer we get.

One of the best advice I've ever received came from a
wise man, Dr. Gary Cook. He told me, "Nick, invest in people, not things. Your life will be more fulfilling." This simple
truth has guided my financial philosophy ever since. Money
can buy things, but it can never buy true joy, meaning, or
fulfillment. Those come from the connections we make, the
lives we touch, and the memories we build.

In economics, consumer debt refers to money owed on
consumable goods—things that depreciate the moment
they're bought. In macroeconomic terms, it's debt that fuels
consumption, not investment. So, while you may be spending, you're not building; you're sinking into a hole that only
gets deeper.

But here's where a shift in perspective can help. Imagine
redirecting the money you would have spent on a fleeting
purchase and investing it in something that truly matters:
your future, your relationships, or a cause that lights your
soul on fire. As Robert Kiyosaki famously said, "It's not how
much money you make, but how much money you help, how
hard it works for you, and how many generations you keep
it for."[65]

Take a step back and consider your financial habits
through a new lens. What do you really want out of life? Is
it more stuff, or is it more time, more freedom, and deeper
connections? Just like that classroom in punctuation, your

perspective can completely transform the meaning of your life.

Dangers of Debt

Let's dive into a powerful case study on the dangers of credit card debt. In 2017, research revealed that two-thirds of Americans (66 percent) were carrying consumer debt, with an average debt load of $34,055 per person.[66] That's a significant number, yet what's more shocking is what happens when you only pay the minimum monthly payments, a path far too many people take.

If an American with $34,055 of credit card debt pays just the minimum each month, the total payments over time would balloon to a staggering $153,487.21. That's more than four and a half times the original balance. Imagine dragging that financial burden for years, working and paying, but never really making a dent. It's a slow bleed, a weight that pulls you down, one statement at a time.

But here's the thing: not all debt is bad. When used wisely, debt can be a powerful tool that helps build wealth. The key is how it's managed.

Think of debt like a well-maintained garden. Good debt, like low-interest loans, is the seeds that, when watered and nurtured, grow into a fruitful harvest. But with its high interest rates, bad debt is like weeds. If left unchecked, it will choke your garden, leaving nothing but financial ruin.

How do you know the difference between good debt and bad debt? The answer lies in one simple principle: Is the interest rate on your debt higher or lower than the potential return on your investments? If the interest rate is higher, it's pulling you further from your financial goals. If it's lower and you're using it to invest in something that grows in value, like real estate or a business, it can be a catalyst for building wealth.

Debt, when used strategically, can be an investment in your future. The goal should always be to eliminate the bad debt—the kind that drags you down with high interest and no return—and focus on leveraging any debt in ways that build your financial future.

By understanding these dynamics and being mindful of where your money is going, you can take control of your financial journey. Like any tool, debt can be used to build or destroy. The choice lies in how you wield it. Apply that wisdom to how you handle debt, and you'll set yourself on a path not just of paying bills but of building wealth.

So, ask yourself: Are you using debt as a tool, or is it using you? The answer can change everything.

Example 1: The Power of Smart Debt

Imagine you have a 3 percent mortgage, and that's considered good debt in today's market. Why? Because opportunities are knocking at your door. Right now, FDIC-insured investments, like Certificates of Deposit (CDs), are offering nearly double that rate. Instead of funneling your extra cash toward paying off your mortgage early, you could double that "net gain" if you put it into a 12 percent-returning investment.

In this scenario, your money is like a well-trained team working behind the scenes, quietly making more money while you focus on living your life. As Warren Buffett said, "If you don't find a way to make money while you sleep, you will work until you die."[67] That's the power of leveraging smart debt.

Example 2: The Burden of Bad Debt

Now, let's shift gears and talk about bad debt. Imagine facing the weight of credit card debt with a sky-high interest rate of 30 percent. This kind of debt can feel like quicksand, pulling you deeper with every passing month. It's not impossible to find investments that return 30 percent or more, but let's be honest: it's rare and risky.

Let's say you have $50,000 in cash. Should you invest it and hope for a return that outpaces that monstrous 30 percent interest rate, or should you pay off the debt? Here's the math: carrying that credit card debt, you're paying $15,000 in interest annually. That's like trying to climb a hill while dragging a boulder behind you. Safe, reliable investments that offer a 30 percent return year after year are few and far between.

The smart decision here is to eliminate the credit card debt. By paying it off, you're not just getting rid of the $15,000 annual burden; you're freeing yourself from the financial chains that hold you back. As Dave Ramsey says, "You can't get out of debt while keeping the same lifestyle that got you there."[68]

In this case, the weight of bad debt can only be lifted by taking decisive action: pay it off and let your financial future breathe a little easier.

Family #1: To Pay Off the Mortgage or Not?

One family approached me with a big question: Should we pay off our mortgage? At first glance, it seemed like a simple financial decision, but as we peeled back the layers of their situation, we discovered the answer wasn't as straightforward as they thought.

They were doing everything right: keeping a healthy budget, living within their means, saving a solid 12 percent of their income, and well on track to retire soon. Their mortgage? A remaining balance of $70,000 with a rock-bottom 3 percent interest rate. On the surface, paying it off was a logical step. But here's where the magic of numbers comes in: their investments consistently performed at over 10 percent a year.

I reminded them of one crucial principle in investing: Past performance doesn't guarantee future returns, but in this case, the odds were in their favor. Interest rates were climbing, and they were earning far more from their investments than they were paying in mortgage interest. After carefully analyzing their financial landscape, the best move for them was not to pay off their mortgage early. Instead, we continued to let their money grow at a higher rate than the 3 percent they were paying in interest. By leveraging smart debt, they were on a fast track toward even greater financial success.

Family #2: The Weight of Bad Debt

Then, another family was weighed down by a mountain of high-interest credit card debt. They were carrying almost $100,000 in credit card balances with interest rates ranging from 19 percent to a staggering 30 percent. Every month, they were pouring $2,500 into these credit card payments, but it felt like they were getting nowhere.

We reviewed their budget and investments, and here was the hard truth: no investment could confidently and consistently return 30 percent annually to outpace that kind of interest. The smart move? Sell off a chunk of their investments to pay off the debt in one fell swoop. I explained that while having a nest egg feels secure, paying off that debt would not only free them from a crushing burden but also allow them to pay themselves the $2,500 they had been spending on credit card companies.

At first, they were reluctant. After all, it's hard to let go of that safety net. But then I showed them the math. At the rate they were going, they'd be paying off credit card debt for decades, and the total interest paid would be astronomical. By selling off investments, paying off the debt, and then re-investing the $2,500 at a reasonable rate of 12 percent, they could turn their financial future around in just a few years.

Within three years, they had rebuilt their wealth to over $100,000, and after 10 years, their account had grown to nearly $600,000. By the time 20 years had passed, they had more than $2.5 million. This is because they made one small change: redirecting their money from paying interest to building wealth. Now, they're living the life they once thought was only a dream.

Family #3: From Debt-Only to Financial Freedom

Another family came to me with a very different situation. They didn't have any investments—only debt. Not all debt is bad, as we already covered, but in this case, they were paying over 20 percent in interest. It was clear their current financial habits wouldn't get them where they wanted to go.

Together, we sat down and reviewed their budget. We found three monthly expenses they could eliminate. One of them, they didn't even realize they were spending money on! Cutting out these unnecessary purchases gave them breathing room to start tackling their debt head-on.

Here's what their debt looked like:

- **Discover Credit Card**: $6,000 at 29 percent interest, monthly payment of $250
- **Student Loan**: $8,000 at 8 percent interest, monthly payment of $250

We developed a plan to attack their highest-interest debt first, using the extra savings from their budget cuts. Every dollar we redirected toward paying their debt was a step toward financial freedom. With determination and focus, they started to see real progress.

The Lesson

Whether dealing with smart debt like a low-interest mortgage or crushing high-interest credit card debt, each family's path to financial freedom is unique. The key is understanding how debt works for or against you and making the necessary changes to put your money where it will grow, not drain.

As Robert Kiyosaki once said, "It's not about how much money you make; it's about how much money you keep, how hard it works for you, and how many generations you keep it for."[69]

Remember, it's not just about the numbers; it's about making thoughtful decisions that will benefit your financial future, your family, and your life goals.

Debt Strategies: The Path to Financial Freedom

When controlling your finances and eliminating debt, consider two powerful strategies: the Debt Snowball Method and the Debt Avalanche Method. Each one takes a unique approach to helping you become debt-free, and choosing the right one can mean the difference between financial stress and financial freedom.

The **Debt Snowball Method** is like building a small snowball at the top of a hill. You start with your smallest debt balance and pay it off as quickly as possible, using any extra income to crush it. Once that debt is paid off, you take the money you were paying and roll it into the next smallest debt, gaining momentum with every step, just like a snowball growing bigger as it rolls downhill. This method is fantastic for motivation. It feels amazing to see those debts disappear one by one.

The **Debt Avalanche Method,** on the other hand, is about maximizing the efficiency of your payments. You start by targeting the debt with the highest interest rate—the bad debt costing you the most. Once that debt is eliminated, you move on to the next highest interest rate, and so on. The logic here is simple: You're tackling the most expensive debt first, saving yourself from wasting money on interest.

Now, the family I worked with was drowning under high-interest credit card debt and student loans. After analyzing their finances, the Debt Avalanche Method was the clear winner for them. Here's how we turned their financial situation around.

We examined their budget closely and identified three small monthly expenses they could eliminate, freeing up $175 a month. In addition, the family was saving $500 a month for retirement. While saving for the future is vital, their current situation called for a shift in priorities: paying off bad debt was the immediate need.

We combined the $175 they had saved by cutting unnecessary expenses with the $500 they were saving, and they suddenly had $675 to put toward paying off their highest-interest debt, on top of the minimum monthly payment of $250. That's $925 monthly toward eliminating the Discover credit card balance, which carried a brutal interest rate of 29 percent.

Within one year, they paid off their Discover credit card entirely. Imagine the relief of watching a balance that once felt insurmountable disappear in just 12 months! But we didn't stop there. With their credit card paid off, they took that $925 a month and turned their attention to their student loans. In just six more months, their student loans were gone as well.

They were completely debt-free, and the only thing they did was make a few small changes to their budget and redirect their money so that it worked smarter, not harder. They went from paying interest to paying themselves, and now they're well on their way to becoming millionaires.

Exercises in Growth

The beauty of these strategies is that they don't require you to make massive, life-altering sacrifices. By analyzing your financial situation, cutting a few unnecessary costs, and rerouting your money to where it can work for you, you can make huge strides toward financial happiness.

Right now, take a moment to reflect on your financial foundation. Ask yourself:

- Are you earning interest or paying it?
- Are your daily financial habits moving you toward wealth, or are you giving away your hard-earned money?

- What small changes can you make today to bring you closer to being Rich by Choice?

• • •

Leverage is the ability to do more with less.
Used wisely, it creates wealth. Used foolishly, it creates ruin.
—Warren Buffett

If you use debt correctly, it can be a powerful tool to build wealth. If debt is using you, it's a financial life of constant struggle in quicksand. Naval Ravikant once stated, "Interest on debt is a tax on our future self."[70] This applies to your money, too. Put it to work for you and make every dollar count.

The path to financial freedom isn't complicated; it's about being intentional with your resources, aligning them with your goals, and making decisions that build your future rather than deplete it. You don't have to be perfect; you just have to be persistent.

The secret to building wealth, paying off debt, and achieving financial freedom is increasing your savings rate. It's as simple as that. Want to get rich faster? Increase your savings rate. Want to get out of debt and finally break free from financial stress? Increase your savings rate. The more you save, the more power you have over your financial future.

The higher your savings rate, the faster you'll pay off debt, build wealth, and reach financial freedom. Every dollar you save is like a seed planted in fertile ground. The more seeds you plant, the bigger your garden of wealth grows. With each increase in your savings rate, you're cultivating a future of abundance and security. The Fundamentals of Money are tried and tested; they work and can work for you. It's time to take control, boost your savings rate, and start accelerating your journey to financial happiness.

To explore resources from this book, scan the QR code or visit RichByChoiceBook.com/bonus.

Nick and Chelsea's Debt Strategies

When Chelsea and I sat down to create our family budget, it was like flipping a switch in our lives. Suddenly, we felt empowered, like we were truly in the driver's seat of our financial future for the first time and on the road to being Rich by Choice. It wasn't just about dollars and cents; it was about taking control of our lives and our destiny. The feeling was transformative. Our budget became the map that guided us toward a life of being Rich by Choice, showing us exactly where we could make small adjustments to align with our dreams and values.

As we worked through the process, something magical happened. We began to feel a sense of peace and freedom we hadn't known before. The future no longer felt like an uncertain fog of "what-ifs" but rather a clear path toward our goals. Little by little, each small change brought us closer to the life we envisioned—one filled with security, joy, and confidence.

The most inspiring part? Knowing that every step, no matter how small, was progress. That sense of forward motion, of being on the right track, infused our lives with happiness. We were no longer worrying about finances; we were excited about the future, energized by the knowledge that we were building something great day by day. This simple act of budgeting gave us the power to design the life we truly wanted and the peace that comes from knowing we were on the path to achieving it.

13

Planning by Choice Chart the Path to Your Desired Destination.

always tell my clients, "We are goal-focused and plan-driven. Our job isn't to predict the future—it's to prepare for it. We hope for the best but build a plan that thrives even in the worst."

That mindset is exactly what Preston and Charlotte needed when they walked into my office, weighed down by anxiety. Preston, especially, was drowning in "what ifs." His thoughts raced with fear—fear of running out of money, fear of market crashes, fear of an uncertain future. He felt like he was one bad break away from losing everything. I could see the burden he carried. So, I asked him to pause, take a deep breath, and trust the process.

I pulled up their financial blueprint on the big screen and walked them through it. Not a vague wish list. Not a loose set of ideas. *A rock-solid, data-backed, deeply personal strategy.* We weren't just planning for tomorrow or next year—we were designing their entire financial future, down to the details.

As we reviewed each section, I saw something incredible happen. Preston's posture shifted. His breathing slowed. Charlotte's eyes lit up with relief. Their stress didn't disappear in an instant, but with each layer of their plan, they saw something they hadn't felt in years: *certainty.*

Here's what we covered:

- **How every dollar of their retirement income was strategically mapped out.** Not just an estimate—an exact plan showing where their income would come from and how it would be sustained.

- **The precise rate of return they actually needed**, not based on market guesses or blind hope, but on their personal goals and lifestyle vision.

- **How inflation—the silent thief of wealth—was already accounted for,** ensuring their money retained its power 20, 30, and even 40 years from now.

- **How we'd create lifelong income without the constant fear of running out,** no matter what the markets or economy threw their way.

- **A crystal-clear projection of their future,** showing them what their wealth would look like in 5, 10, 20, and 30 years.

- **The life they could actually afford to live.** How much more could they spend freely, without guilt or fear, while still securing their future?

- **Their legacy strategy.** How they'd pass wealth, values, and impact to their children—not just money, but a meaningful inheritance. It is called an "Effective and Efficient Transfer." What is the fastest and least costly way to pass your assets to your loved ones? What are strategies to protect your family and eliminate/reduce estate taxes?

- **A plan for the unexpected.** Market crashes, healthcare costs, economic downturns—we had a contingency for all of it. No surprises. No panic. Just preparedness.

- **The fine print that matters.** Social Security strategies, tax planning, required minimum distributions (RMDs), and risk management—it was all optimized to work for them, not against them.

I ran their plan through every extreme scenario we could imagine. What if the market crashed the day they retired? What if inflation skyrocketed? What if a major health crisis drained their savings?

The result? Their plan held strong. Preston and Charlotte weren't just financially secure—they were fortified.

The Hard Truth About Financial Uncertainty

Most people live in financial reaction mode, hoping things work out, praying they won't hit a crisis, and crossing their fingers that they won't run out of money. But hope is not a strategy. It is more peaceful to be proactive rather than reactive. *A plan is.*

Your financial future doesn't have to be a guessing game. It can be a well-structured, resilient roadmap—a plan that isn't just built to last but built to win.

The Questions You Can't Ignore

- Are you living with financial confidence—or financial anxiety?
- Do you have a plan that works for every season of life—or just for right now?
- If the unexpected happened tomorrow, would you be prepared—or would it shake everything?
- Are you maximizing your money's potential—or leaving opportunities on the table?
- Are you designing your financial future—or leaving it up to chance?

The choice is yours. *Financial stress is optional.* But so is financial confidence.

Which will you choose?

A Financial Plan Stress Test

The cherry on top was that we conducted a complete stress test analysis. A financial plan stress test is an evaluation process designed to simulate how a financial plan would perform under various extreme conditions, ensuring both catastrophe preparedness and the maximization of future opportunities.

It examines how your financial strategies withstand unexpected disruptions, such as severe market downturns, job loss, health crises, or economic shifts. It also identifies ways to capitalize on potential financial opportunities, such as high-potential growth investments or tax optimization strategies.

Planning for Catastrophe

In the context of catastrophe planning, a stress test assesses how your finances would handle worst-case scenarios. It evaluates:

- **Loss of Income**: What happens if you or your spouse loses your job?
- **Market Crashes**: How would your investments and retirement savings withstand a market downturn or recession?
- **Health Emergencies**: Do you have enough insurance or savings in place to cover medical emergencies or disability?
- **Inflation/Interest Rate Spikes**: How vulnerable are you to sudden economic changes?
- **Wealth Protection**: This refers to the strategies and measures used to safeguard your assets and financial resources from potential risks, such as lawsuits, taxes, inflation, or economic downturns. The goal is to enhance and protect your wealth over time.
- **Wealth transfer**: The process of passing on your assets, such as property, investments, or money, to your heirs or beneficiaries, typically through strategic estate planning.

The goal is to ensure you have adequate protection to withstand unexpected shocks without disrupting your long-term goals.

Maximizing Future Opportunities

On the other hand, a financial stress test can reveal how your plan could perform under favorable conditions or help you identify opportunities to grow your wealth further. It evaluates:

- **Investment Opportunities**: What could happen if your investment portfolio exceeds expectations? How will you rebalance?

- **Proactive Tax Strategies**: Are you positioned to minimize taxes in the future through strategies like tax-loss harvesting, asset location, or Roth conversions?

- **Growth Scenarios**: How can you capitalize on market upswings, real estate booms, or advancements in your career?

By stress-testing both the downside risks and potential upsides, you ensure your financial plan is resilient and flexible, designed to protect you in bad times while allowing you to seize opportunities in good times.

We addressed every fear Preston had with a solid, well-thought-out plan. We weren't just throwing darts in the dark; we were shining a light on every shadowy concern.

Something incredible happened as we reviewed their plan. Preston, who had come in with his shoulders hunched under the weight of stress, began to relax. Slowly, that anxiety turned into peace. By the end of our meeting, he was smiling, and his whole demeanor had shifted. He looked at me and said, "I was so silly for worrying. That was wasted time and energy." It was as if a massive boulder had been lifted from his shoulders. That's the power of planning.

Planning transforms the unknown into the known. It replaces fear with clarity and anxiety with confidence. Planning allows us to see the opportunities even in the face of life's uncertainties.

In the midst of chaos, there is also opportunity.

—Sun Tzu

Using the Pillars of a Great Financial Plan

A truly great financial plan stands on three pillars: Great Investments, Great planning, and Great Discipline. It's not enough to hope things work out. A good plan answers critical questions.

- When will we get there?
- How will we get there?
- Do we have enough?
- Are we on track?
- What do we need to adjust along the way?
- What unexpected events could derail us?
- And the biggest question of all: Will we ever run out of money?

You should never have to live with that nagging question in the back of your mind. A solid financial plan brings comfort and confidence because you'll know the answers.

Right now, take a moment to think about your own financial plan. Can you answer these questions? If not, that's okay, but it's an area to work on. Software, tools, and expert guidance are available to help you get there.

• • •

As Benjamin Franklin wisely said, "By failing to prepare, you are preparing to fail." Make sure your plan guides you toward the life you truly want. With the right strategy, you can reach your financial goals *and* enjoy the journey along the way with peace of mind.

To explore resources from this book, scan the QR code or visit RichByChoiceBook.com/bonus.

Nick and Chelsea's Plan

Planning a Life of Purpose, Joy, and Legacy

Some people let life happen to them. Chelsea and I try to design ours.

Late at night, when the house is finally quiet and the kids are asleep, Chelsea and I sit down with a notebook and look at the future laid out before us. We plan not just for the next year but for the next five, ten, or fifty years. Our conversations aren't just about numbers on a page; they are about dreams, experiences, and the life we want to build together. We don't just ask, *"What do we need?"*—we ask, *"What do we want to feel? What memories do we want to create?"*

We try to make planning fun. We plan for family adventures, knowing that the joy of discovery—new cities, cultures, and experiences—will shape our children's worldviews. We talk about our kids' futures, ensuring that when the time comes, their college education is a choice, not a burden. We even dream about the day we'll walk our daughters down the aisle, knowing that those moments, though fleeting, will be priceless.

But one of the most meaningful things I've been focusing on lately is what I call "Lasting Activities." These are not just hobbies; they are threads woven into the fabric of our family for a lifetime. So many activities—like sports, games, or even certain traditions—fade with age, but what can we do together for the next 50 years? What can we invest in today that will bring us joy, connection, and laughter for decades to come?

Dancing. Singing. Playing music. Swimming. These are things that don't expire with time but instead grow richer as the years pass. I imagine us, years from now, dancing at our grandchildren's weddings, playing guitar by a campfire, and laughing as we swim together on summer vacations. These aren't just hobbies—they are legacies of love.

Life goes by quickly, and before we know it, another year has vanished amidst the busyness of daily routines and endless responsibilities. One powerful way to reclaim peace in the midst of this busyness is through automation in financial planning. By automating your financial strategies—such as savings, investments, and retirement contributions—you free yourself from constant decision-making, stress, and worry.

Automation provides comfort and clarity, ensuring your financial goals are continuously being met behind the scenes and allowing you to fully immerse yourself in the meaningful moments of everyday life. You'll find peace knowing your future is secured without the burden of constant vigilance. This peace empowers you to be present, soaking in each precious moment, enjoying the swiftly passing years with your loved ones, confident that your financial foundation is firmly in place.

Life isn't just about accumulating wealth—it's about intentionally crafting the moments that make wealth worth having. Chelsea and I plan not just to secure our financial future but to ensure that our time, our love, and our joy multiply with every passing year. Because in the end, it's not just about what we leave behind—it's about the life we choose to live... together.

14

Protection by Choice
Knowledge Reduces Risks, Helping You Build Wealth that Lasts Beyond a Lifetime.

Charlie and Susan were clients who had built a beautiful life together. They had three children—two sons and a daughter—each a reflection of the love and joy that filled their home. But one day, far too soon, Charlie was taken from this earth. I'll never forget the moment I got the call. My body froze, my breath caught in my chest, and my mind refused to believe it. But it was true. Charlie was gone.

The funeral was a sea of heartbreak. Faces twisted in grief, eyes swollen with tears, and the air thick with the weight of loss. What do you say when words fail? How do you comfort children whose world has been shattered? There's no fixing such a deep, profound wound. My heart aches for them still.

Yet, in the midst of that unimaginable pain, there was one small light: We had a plan. Charlie had been the primary earner for the family, and that income was now gone. But the strategy we had built together—through careful planning—ensured that while they couldn't bring Charlie back, they could keep their lives together. The financial stability gave them the freedom to grieve and heal and to face each day without the crushing weight of financial ruin.

Would they trade it all for just one more day with Charlie? Of course. But that plan allowed them to move forward as a family without the suffocating pressure of financial stress, and that is a priceless gift in such a devastating time.

The True Meaning of Financial Protection

Let's be clear: financial protection is not just about insurance. Yes, insurance can play a critical role, but protection is broader: it's about planning for the unexpected. Life is unpredictable, and while we can't foresee every storm, we can build a shelter strong enough to withstand it.

As you assess your finances, here are some tough but vital questions to ask yourself:

- What would my family do if my spouse or I passed away today?
- What plan do we have if my spouse or I become unemployed or experience a reduced income?
- What if I became disabled, or one of us faced a severe illness?

These questions may feel uncomfortable, but they are essential. As much as we'd like to think, "That will never happen to me," I've seen firsthand that life can change in an instant. I often tell my clients, "My job is to hope for the best but plan for the worst." It's a hard truth, but the families that plan are the ones who can weather life's storms.

What Does Your Protection Plan Look Like?

Do you have a plan to safeguard your family if the unthinkable happens? If not, now is the time to start building one. Yes, there are insurance products that can help, but the answer isn't always "more insurance." Sometimes, you need a solid plan, one that includes emergency savings, diversified investments, and strategies for reducing expenses when life takes an unexpected turn.

For instance, if my spouse lost their job unexpectedly, we have a plan that would allow us to cut our budget by 25 percent if necessary. We could adjust our lifestyle, knowing we have options to protect ourselves from financial hardship. It's not about avoiding risk entirely; it's about creating a strategy to handle whatever life throws at us.

> *A goal without a plan is just a wish.*
> —Antoine de Saint-Exupery.

> *The future depends on what we do in the present.*
> —Mahatma Gandhi

Don't wait for a life-altering event to wake up to the need for protection. Build your plan now so that your family will be secure no matter what happens.

Take a moment today to review your finances.

- What strategies and investments do you currently have to protect your family from the unexpected?
- If you don't have a plan yet, what steps can you take to implement one?

A solid financial plan isn't just about accumulating wealth; it's about protecting what you've built and ensuring that your family can thrive no matter the challenges life brings.

The Gift That Keeps Giving: Building a Legacy and Passing Down Wisdom, Not Just Wealth

At Michels Family Financial, we recognize the profound responsibility and opportunity that comes with passing wealth to future generations. That's why we've dedicated an entire area within our Elite Wealth Management Formula to "FRM," or Family Relationship Management.

THE WEALTH MANAGEMENT FORMULA

WM = IC + AP + RM

IC = INVESTMENT CONSULTING

WM (Wealth Management) =

IC
(Investment Consulting)
+ AP
(Advanced Planning)
+ RM
(Relationship Management)

Management of all investment elements to maximize the probability of clients achieving all that is important to them.

➤ Portfolio performance analysis
➤ Risk evaluation
➤ Asset allocation
➤ Assessment of impact of costs
➤ Assessment of impact of taxes
➤ Investment policy statement

AP = WE + WT + WP + CG

RM = CRM + PNRM + FRM

AP (Advanced Planning) =

WE
(Wealth Enhancement: tax mitigation and cash-flow planning)
+ WT
(Wealth Transfer: transferring wealth effectively; may not be within a family)
+ WP
(Wealth Protection: risk mitigation, legal structures and transferring risk to insurance company)
+ CG
(Charitable Giving: maximizing charitable impact)

RM (Relationship Management)
= CRM
(Client Relationship Management)
+ PNRM
(Professional Network Relationship Management)
+ FRM
(Family Relationship Management)

This pillar is thoughtfully designed to help families educate, equip, and empower their loved ones, successfully preparing their family's future generations to manage inheritance wisely and responsibly. Our mission is rooted in a deep passion: to see the wealth you've built serve as a springboard—one that enhances your family's future, enriches their lives, and creates lasting legacies for generations to come.

Passing on wealth to our children and loved ones should be one of life's most meaningful acts of love. However, without preparation, it can unintentionally cause more harm than good. Proven research shows that the first generation wastes most of its inheritance in the United States and is almost entirely depleted by the second generation. These heartbreaking statistics are often referred to as "shirt sleeve to shirt sleeve."

As parents, this hits close to home—our children are our greatest joy, and their future is our most important legacy. We want them to experience lives filled with love, laughter, peace, and happiness. While also being equipped with the wisdom and knowledge to handle the gifts we've worked so hard to provide. Imagine the joy of looking down from heaven and seeing the wealth we passed on used as a springboard to elevate their lives and their loved ones.

The good news? We can break the cycle and ensure our wealth becomes a lasting blessing. Research shows that 85 percent of inheritance-related failures can be prevented with just two crucial strategies: financial literacy and empowerment.

Strategy 1: Teaching About Money

The first step is teaching our children and grandchildren about money. Not leaving it up to chance or relying on others. Financial literacy is the foundation for making wise decisions, and as parents, it's our role to teach and lead by example. Through structured, life-stage-specific education, like the programs we offer at Michels Family Financial, we can provide tailored lessons that grow with them, from basic budgeting for teens to understanding investments and wealth-building as adults.

More information is available at MichelsFamilyCorporation.com or by scanning the QR code below.

Strategy 2: Less Control, More Empowerment

The second key to success is less control and more empowerment. Too often, conversations about inheritance are limited to a brief mention of legal arrangements, leaving children unprepared for the responsibility. Instead, imagine an ongoing dialogue where you show your children what they will inherit, share the story of how you built it, and ask them how they would manage it when it becomes theirs. Listen to their thoughts, encourage their ideas, and give them space to learn from mistakes under your guidance. Speak from the heart, not from authority. Let them understand that the wealth they will receive is not just about money—it's about the values, habits, and faith that built it.

If you can accomplish these two things with your kids (Financial Literacy and Less Control, More Empowerment), then that alleviates 85 percent of the problem. Here are four simple and easy steps to help.

Step 1: Foster Open Communication

Research shows that the more open you are with your children about finances and inheritance, the better their chances of success. Hiding details or waiting until the last minute often leads to confusion and poor outcomes. If your children are going to inherit something down the road, the sooner they know, the longer they have to prepare, and the better prepared they'll be to handle it responsibly. Open communication builds trust, encourages transparency, and fosters a sense of readiness. Don't view these discussions as one-time events; instead, make them ongoing and evolving conversations that grow along with your family.

Step 2: Empower, Don't Just Inform

Instead of simply telling your children what they will inherit, empower them to take ownership of it. This can be as simple as saying, "Let me show you what you're going to inherit. Now, if this were yours today, what would you do with it?" Then, pause and listen. Encourage them to think critically and come up with their own ideas. Empowering them in this way helps them develop confidence and decision-making skills. By involving them in these conversations early, you're giving them the opportunity to understand their inheritance and how it fits into their long-term goals.

Step 3: Share the Journey Behind the Wealth

Wealth is more than a number—it's a story of hard work, sacrifice, values, and blessings. Take time to share this journey with your children: "We'd like to tell you how we built this wealth and educate you on the core values, beliefs, and habits that made it possible. Next to God's blessings, these values are the reason for our success." Some families even plan dedicated family vacations or retreats around this experience. Consider using this time to create a family mission statement or purpose statement for the wealth. Set actionable goals and develop plans that reflect your family's shared vision. At a minimum, prioritize regular discussions about the purpose and responsibilities that come with wealth.

Step 4: Speak from the Heart, Not from Authority

When discussing inheritance, approach the conversation with love and sincerity, not authority. Share your hopes and dreams for your children: "It would give us immense joy to look down from heaven and see you use this inheritance—gifts from God and blessings we worked hard to build—as a springboard to elevate your life and those you love. We don't want to see it drained or wasted, but instead used to create a future of financial peace, security, and happiness." Help them understand that wealth can be a tremendous blessing but also a potential burden if mishandled. Let them know that because you love them, you want to help prepare them for this responsibility. Speaking from the heart fosters deeper understanding, strengthens emotional connections, and inspires a lasting legacy.

• • •

When passed with purpose, wealth can be a springboard to elevate future generations and bless them with financial peace and security. But when left to chance, it often becomes a burden or a missed opportunity. Let's embrace this responsibility now with open communication, family mission statements, and meaningful discussions. Let's give our children the tools they need to grow what we've built and create legacies of their own. What a beautiful gift it would be to see our children use our blessings as a foundation for lives filled with purpose, joy, and gratitude. The future of your family is worth the effort today.

To explore resources from this book, scan the QR code or visit RichByChoiceBook.com/bonus.

Nick and Chelsea: Reducing Risks, Planning for the Future, Protecting Legacy

Perfect for Kids and Grandkids

Chelsea and I are not just teaching our kids about money—we are trying to create a legacy of financial empowerment, resilience, and joy that I hope they'll carry throughout their lives. One of our favorite tools in this journey has been the engaging and educational board game "Cash Flow," inspired by Robert Kiyosaki's classic book "Rich Dad Poor Dad." The game provides each player with a detailed profile card outlining their job, income, assets, liabilities, and monthly expenses. Players then strategize to purchase assets such as real estate, stocks, businesses, and other income-producing investments. The ultimate goal? Achieving financial independence by generating passive income greater than their day-to-day living expenses, allowing them to leave the "rat race" and quit their day jobs.

The original "Cash Flow" game is perfect for older kids and adults, offering complex scenarios that teach strategic investing, risk management, and entrepreneurial thinking. We have even made some fun adjustments to the game to make it more fun and to highlight the concepts and strategies we are currently focusing on.

Its junior version simplifies these principles into playful scenarios suitable for younger kids, gently introducing concepts like earning, spending wisely, and saving. Through both games, our kids are learning invaluable life skills: critical thinking, creativity, patience, and confidence. More importantly, they are discovering how to master money as a powerful tool to create an incredible life filled with freedom, choice, and purpose.

We bought these games and let them collect dust for about a year before we finally cracked them open. Life moves fast, and intentions don't always translate into immediate actions. I'm far from perfect, but our commitment to being good parents keeps us moving forward. Maybe you're similar. We might not always get it right on the first try, but as long as we're striving to do our best and build meaningful legacies for our children, we're doing something incredibly special.

15

Compounding by Choice
Take Small Steps Today to Shape Your Legacy.

There are moments in life that change everything. For two young women, it was the day their mother, a powerful and wealthy businesswoman, was told she had only a few months left to live.[71] Though her heart ached, her mind was clear—she wanted to leave her daughters with more than just money. She wanted to gift them with a choice, a lesson, and the opportunity to live their lives fully, with wisdom guiding them.

"If I could, I would give you both the world," she said to her two daughters, her voice soft but full of emotion. "But what I can give you is a gift that will help you navigate the world, and it comes with a choice."

There were two luxurious Louis Vuitton bags on the table beside her. One was filled with a staggering $1,000,000, the crisp bills neatly stacked and gleaming under the light. The other held only a shiny penny, glowing as if imbued with magic.

"You can choose the million dollars or the penny," their mother said with a smile, her eyes flickering with love and wisdom. "But know this: Whatever you choose will remain under my manager's care for one month. If you choose the penny, the amount will double each day you leave it untouched. The million, however, can be borrowed from my bank if you wish. The choice is yours. Take the night to think it over, and come to me tomorrow with your decision." She kissed each daughter tenderly, handing them both a small, worn book titled *The Power to Choose*. "Remember," she said, "your choice shapes your future."

That night, the first daughter couldn't sleep. She lay in bed, her mind racing. *Why would Mother offer us a single penny? Surely, the million dollars is the smarter choice,* she thought. Frustrated, she reached for the book her mother had given her and opened it to the first story.

In the story, a tiny water hyacinth dreamed of crossing the vast pond, but its tiny size made the journey seem impossible. Each day, the water laughed at the hyacinth's dream. But the water didn't know that the hyacinth had a secret: It could double in size every day.

The first month this little water hyacinth appeared, nobody noticed it. By month fifteen, it had reproduced to cover barely one square foot of water. In month twenty, only one person passing by the pond noticed the little patch of foliage floating off to the side but mistook it for a large bath towel or perhaps a discarded piece of wrapping paper. In month twenty-nine, half the pond's surface was still open water. By the next month, the entire pond was covered by a rich blanket of purple-pink flowers, transforming the once-empty waters into a lush, living carpet of beauty.

The girl closed the book, suddenly realizing the connection between the story and her mother's offer: *the penny. It doubled like the hyacinth.*

Meanwhile, the second daughter had made up her mind the moment their mother placed the million-dollar bag in front of her. She was ready to get rich quickly and wasted no time the next morning, choosing the million and setting up meetings with financial advisors and business strategists to turn her windfall into an empire.

The first daughter, however, returned quietly to her mother and chose the penny. She understood now. This wasn't just about wealth; it was about the power of patience, compounding growth, and the long game.

By the end of the second week, the first daughter's collection of pennies had grown to just shy of ninety dollars ($81.92, to be exact). It wasn't much, certainly not enough to cover a nice dinner in the city where her sister's financial team worked tirelessly to make more of her million. A few days into the third week, her seemingly humble penny had blossomed into a sum of $655.35. Still modest by her sister's standards, the girl was content, her eyes twinkling with confidence.

Patience is the key to unlocking unimaginable wealth.

The second daughter scoffed, mocking her sister's decision. "I can't believe you went for the penny!" she exclaimed, laughing off the idea as foolish. But the girl who had chosen the penny wouldn't be swayed by doubt or ridicule. She knew something her sister did not: Patience is the key to unlocking unimaginable wealth.

As the month marched on and the mother died, the second sister's world took a turn. Her executive director delivered grim news: the markets had soured, and those golden projections she had counted on were now a distant memory. She tried to maintain her composure, but the cracks in her voice betrayed her growing worry as she waited for more updates.

On the morning of day 31, the executive director returned, the moment both sisters had been waiting for. His expression was serious, his tone somber. He shuffled nervously, cleared his throat, and requested a glass of water before delivering his report. "The good news," he began hesitantly, addressing the second daughter, "is that some investments did okay. There's been a modest gain."

The girl sighed with relief but quickly tensed again as she braced for the rest. "And the bad news?" she asked, her voice barely a whisper.

The director wiped his brow and looked down. "Well, after expenses—commissions, taxes, broker fees, the corporate office rent, interest on the credit line, and, of course, my fee…" He trailed off as the color drained from the girl's face. "You're $250,000 in debt."

The director turned to the first daughter and said, "On day 28, your penny surpassed the million-dollar mark. By day 29, it had grown to a staggering two and a half million. And today," he continued as he turned to the bags behind him. The manager handed her a luxurious Louis Vuitton bag, filled to the brim.

Unsure what to say, the first daughter opened the bag. The number that greeted her was nothing short of mind-blowing: $10,737,418.24. It all began with one tiny, insignificant little penny.

The first daughter had unlocked one of the most powerful forces known to man, often called "The eighth wonder of the world"—the incredible, unstoppable force of compound interest. This was the same phenomenon that spread a single water hyacinth to blanket an entire pond. Meanwhile, the second daughter, who had chased the allure of quick wealth, stood there devastated and penniless, a victim of her impatience.

The lesson was clear: the path to true wealth doesn't lie in shortcuts or instant gratification. It lies in understanding the extraordinary power of time, growth, and the quiet, steady magic/power of compounding. In the end, the daughter who trusted in the power of compounding not only inherited her mother's wealth but also her wisdom, while the other learned the hard truth that quick riches often come at a great cost. The power to choose is yours—will you chase immediate gratification, or will you invest in the patient, steady growth that leads to extraordinary abundance?

The Lesson of Patience and Compound Growth

Compound interest is the world's eighth wonder.
He who understands it earns it...
He who doesn't, pays it.

—Albert Einstein

This story reminds us that the power to choose lies within us, and sometimes, the most insignificant-seeming option can lead to unimaginable wealth if we give it time to grow.

Warren Buffett once said, "The stock market is a device for transferring money from the impatient to the patient."[72] Whether it's a penny or a portfolio, the key is to trust in the process, stay the course, and let time work its magic. You, too, have the power to choose.

The Gift of Wisdom

Small deeds done are better than great deeds planned.
—Peter Marshall

When the wealthy mother in our story offered her daughters a gift, one daughter saw only money. The other daughter, however, recognized something much deeper—*wisdom*. This mother wasn't just passing on a fortune; she was teaching her daughters a timeless truth: *the power of compounding*. The lesson wasn't just about money. It was about life. The mother lovingly taught her daughters that compounding doesn't just transform wealth—it transforms lives. The little things, done consistently, create the biggest impact.

Applying the Power of Compounding to Your Life

Here's the secret of compounding: You must start *right now*. It doesn't matter if you're young or older, whether you're looking back with regret or forward with hope—the only thing that matters is today. Time is like sand slipping through your fingers. Blink, and the years will pass by.

Think about where you want to be in five, ten, or twenty years. Do you want to be in the same place you are now? Or do you want to be living the life you've dreamed of? The faster you start, the faster you'll be on the road to financial freedom. Don't delay. Start today. Make a plan and put the magic of compounding to work for you.

You must start *right now*.

The Discipline of Compounding: How the Wealthy Leverage It

Once you understand the power of compounding, the next step is cultivating the discipline and patience to let it work. Compounding rewards those willing to wait—those who let their wealth grow slowly but surely over time.

Charlie Munger, Buffett's longtime partner, adds to this with his philosophy on *opportunity cost*. Every decision we make—saving or spending, investing or not—has an opportunity cost. The wealthy understand this deeply, making calculated decisions based on what they stand to gain over time.

The Problem Isn't How Much You Make—It's How You Use It

> *You don't have to be rich to start,*
> *but you have to start to be rich.*
> —Zig Ziglar

The true power of wealth lies not in how much you earn but in what you do with it. Compounding is the quiet, steady engine that transforms your financial future, but only if you let it. So, whether you're young and just starting or older and thinking it's too late, it's never too late to harness the power of compounding and build the life you've always wanted. Start today. The power to change your future is in your hands, one penny at a time.

The Power to Choose Your Future

The best time to plant a tree was 20 years ago.
The second-best time is today.

—Chinese Proverb

Right now, you hold the power to choose your future. Whether you want to be wealthy, wise, or build meaningful relationships, the process is the same: make small, intentional decisions today and let them grow over time. Imagine for a moment: What if you committed to reading just 10 pages of a book every day? Over time, you'd accumulate vast knowledge. Or, what if you saved and invested 10 percent of your income? Your future wealth would be substantial.

It doesn't matter if you're 20, 40, or 70. The magic lies in starting *today*. Time will pass regardless, and you have a choice—*will you let that time work for you or against you?*

How the Wealthy Use Compounding

The wealthy know this secret well. The rich don't chase quick returns. They understand that true wealth comes from allowing time to compound their efforts and investments.

Charlie Munger says, "Intelligent people make decisions based on opportunity cost."[73] Every choice you make today—what you spend your money on, where you invest your time—has a cost. Those who are Rich by Choice grasp this deeply, choosing paths that may require patience but yield the highest returns.

Small Decisions, Big Outcomes

*Success is nothing more than a few simple disciplines
practiced every day.*

—Jim Rohn

If I walked up to you today and offered $3 million to quit a harmful habit, would you do it? What if I told you that skipping that $7 daily coffee, soda, or cigarette, or canceling a couple of the monthly subscriptions you never use and don't realize you're still paying for, could amount to millions over the course of your life if invested wisely? Let's break it down. A pack of cigarettes costs around $7, and a few sodas can add up to $5. That's $12 a day that, if saved and invested at 12 percent over the course of your life, could grow into *millions*. It's not about how much money you make; it's about *where* your money goes.

The power of compounding doesn't require you to earn more—it simply asks that you make better decisions with what you already have. Your habits, whether financial, emotional, or physical, are the building blocks of your future. What you choose to do today will dictate where you are in five, ten, or twenty years.

Small, consistent choices—like cutting unnecessary expenses—can have monumental impacts. Compounding is a slow build, like planting seeds in a garden. At first, you might not see the growth, but with patience and care, your garden flourishes, eventually blooming into something magnificent.

You Have the Power to Choose Your Future

Your habits will determine your future.
—Jack Canfield

You have the ability to change your life right now. The incredible power of compounding involves every area of your life. Whether you want to be wealthier, smarter, or happier, it all starts with one simple choice. Every day, you're presented with opportunities to build the future you desire.

Let's play the *"What If"* game. Circle all that resonate with you:

- **What if, starting right now,** you committed to reading just 10 pages of a good book every day? Over time, you'd become a well of knowledge and insight, far smarter than you are today.

- **What if, starting right now,** you decided to save and invest 10 percent of your income? That small habit, over years, could lead to financial independence.

- **What if, starting right now,** you made a point to share a heartfelt compliment with a loved one each day? Can you imagine the depth and warmth of your relationships in the years to come?

- **What if, starting right now,** you made it a daily habit to say words of love right before you walked out your front door every morning and the first thing you did when you entered your front door every afternoon? Can you imagine how your relationships would flourish with this simple act of love and kindness?

- **What if, starting right now,** you dedicated just 15 minutes a day to physical exercise? Over time, those minutes would compound into better health, more energy, and a stronger body.

- **What if, starting right now,** you practiced gratitude every morning by writing down three things you're thankful for? It could shift your mindset and lead to a more joyful, fulfilled life.

- **What if, starting right now,** you reduced screen time by an hour each day and used that time to learn a new skill or pursue a passion? Imagine the progress you'd make in a year.

- **What if, starting right now,** you focused on eating one healthy meal a day? Over time, it would dramatically improve your overall well-being and energy levels.

- **What if, starting right now,** you set aside time each week to call or visit a family member or friend? Those small moments could strengthen your bonds and create lasting memories.

- **What if, starting right now,** you set a daily goal to learn something new—whether it's a fact, a skill, or a new perspective? In a year, you'd be a reservoir of knowledge.

- **What if, starting right now,** you spent a few minutes each evening reflecting on your day's accomplishments and identifying small improvements for tomorrow? Over time, this habit of reflection could skyrocket your personal growth and self-awareness.

- **What if, starting right now,** you spent 15 minutes every day reflecting on gratitude and appreciating the little things in life? Imagine how this shift in mindset would fill your days with positivity, increasing happiness and well-being.

- **What if, starting right now,** you decided to reduce or eliminate one bad habit, like excessive sugar consumption or procrastination? The ripple effects of this decision could transform your health or productivity.

- **What if, starting right now,** you made it a habit to set aside time each day to meditate or reflect? Over time, this would give you clarity, reduce stress, and enhance your sense of peace.

- **What if, starting right now,** you made a conscious effort to listen more in conversations? You'd likely build deeper, more meaningful connections with others.

- **What if, starting right now,** you spent 10 minutes each night planning for the next day? Over time, you'll notice improved productivity, focus, and a sense of accomplishment.

You see, your life is not defined by a single moment but by the accumulation of small decisions made consistently over time. The person you want to become, the life you want to live, is within reach—but only if you start now. This applies not just to money but to every area of your life.

The power to change your life, to achieve financial happiness and personal fulfillment, is already within you. But you must start now. Don't wait. The magic of compounding—whether it's with your money, your relationships, or your personal growth—will transform your life if you let it.

The journey to financial happiness begins today. It's time to make your choice.

Your Daily Habits Create Your Destiny

Success is the sum of small efforts,
repeated day in and day out.
—Robert Collier

Take a moment to reflect on your life. What kind of future do you want? Who do you want to be? Write it down—every dream, every goal—and then identify one small action you can start today. Whether saving a little more, investing in your knowledge, or nurturing your relationships, each step counts.

It's time to create new habits that will positively shape your future. Your habits, both financial and personal, will dictate your level of success and happiness. This is a quick exercise, but the value is immeasurable.

1. Take a moment and write down your goals—the person you want to be, the life you want to live, the financial world you want to experience…
2. Next to each goal, write down one small, daily action that will move you toward that vision.
3. Take small actions every day. They will compound, shaping your future.

It won't happen overnight, but it *will* happen. The power of compounding, the power of daily choices, is the secret to creating the life of your dreams. You have the ability to shape your future, achieve financial happiness, cultivate fulfilling relationships, and build a legacy that lasts.

How exciting is that? You have the power to determine your future. You can accomplish all of your goals and live the life you've always dreamed of—but you must start right now. Don't wait. Every day is a new opportunity to let the magic of compounding work in your favor. Your future is in your hands. Embrace it, and let the power of compounding guide you toward a life of abundance and joy.

• • •

You see, your life is not defined by a single moment but by the accumulation of small decisions made consistently over time. The person you want to become, the life you want to live, is within reach—but only if you start now. This applies not just to money but to every area of your life.

What if you started today? What future could you create?

To explore resources from this book, scan the QR code or visit RichByChoiceBook.com/bonus.

Nick and Chelsea's Lasting Family Activities

Embracing intentionality profoundly transformed my life, revealing an entirely new perspective filled with clarity and purpose. When I discovered the incredible power behind the single word "intentional," I began approaching every aspect of my life differently. No longer drifting through the days, I took a deliberate pause to deeply consider every vital area of my life—Faith, Family, Relationships, Financial Health, Business, Personal Growth, Reading and Education, Health and Wellness.

Each reflection illuminated the path toward the life I truly desired, guiding me to ask critical questions: What's working well? What needs improvement? What would each category look like in an ideal world? From these reflections emerged simple, actionable steps to steadily shape the life of my dreams. As John C. Maxwell wisely stated, "You will never change your life until you change something you do daily. The secret of your success is found in your daily routine."

This specific exercise sparked an amazing revelation in my life. I created what I call "Lasting Activities." I realized the importance of intentionally choosing hobbies and interests that my family and I could share indefinitely. When my oldest son turned 18 and headed off to college, it highlighted that while coaching youth sports, playing in sports leagues, and endless hours of throwing the baseball or football together were wonderful, these activities had a limited timeframe. Inspired by these memories, I started intentionally seeking activities we could enjoy together, whether we were 45 or 95.

This intentional approach deeply enriched my relationships and family life. It did not happen overnight, but by intentionally and closely observing my children's interests, I asked myself, "What could be lasting?"

I joined the swim team with my daughter, transforming her passion into cherished memories. I stepped out of my comfort zone to learn cheerleading stunts, creating priceless moments of trust and teamwork with another daughter. With my son, I started guitar lessons, forging a lifelong bond through music.

With my wife, I intentionally engaged in dance lessons, spiritual growth, and shared reading, recognizing that nurturing our partnership profoundly strengthened every other aspect of our lives. This list can go on: traveling, pickleball, swimming, and exploring real estate and business opportunities.

These "Lasting Activities" weren't about mastery, but the intentional pursuit of these activities has created deeper connections and enriched our family bond profoundly.

Honestly, I don't know exactly how this journey will turn out, but the process itself has been incredibly fun and fulfilling. Though I am not good—in fact, I am terrible at some—I am having fun trying and learning new things. The great silver lining: quality time with the people I love most. What is better than that? All of this is inspired by being intentional and the incredible power of compounding.

Here's a simple 3-step process I used to bring intentionality into every aspect of my life:

1. **List Your Life Categories:**

    o   Faith
    o   Family
    o   Relationships
    o   Financial Health
    o   Business
    o   Personal Growth
    o   Reading and Education
    o   Health and Wellness

2. **Reflect and Question:** For each category, ask:

    o   How satisfied am I with this area?
    o   What's going well? What's challenging?
    o   What specific changes would make this area better?
    o   In an ideal scenario, how does this part of my life look and feel?

3. **Simple, Actionable Steps:**

    o   **Faith:** Spend 5 minutes each morning in quiet reflection or prayer. Benefit: Brings daily clarity, peace, and a deeper sense of purpose.

- **Family:** Dedicate one evening each week to family activities without distractions. Benefit: Strengthens family bonds and creates lasting memories.

- **Relationships:** Regularly reach out to someone you care about with a simple message or call. Benefit: Deepens connections and fosters ongoing support.

- **Financial Health:** Automate savings or investment contributions monthly. Benefit: Creates financial security and reduces stress.

- **Business:** Commit to 10 minutes daily of strategic planning or goal review. Benefit: Keeps you focused, organized, and effective.

- **Personal Growth:** Journal daily about gratitude or progress. Benefit: Boosts confidence, resilience, and motivation.

- **Reading and Education:** Read at least 10 pages of a book every day. Benefit: Stimulates continuous learning and creativity and broadens perspectives.

- **Health and Wellness**: Walk or stretch for at least 10 minutes daily. Benefit: Improves overall health, energy, and emotional well-being.

By taking these simple, intentional steps daily, you'll harness the profound power of compounding, transforming your dreams into reality, one meaningful action at a time.

16

Investing by Choice Win the Game by Mastering the Rules.

Many years ago, a lovely couple named Doug and Brittany came into my office. They were hard-working, down-to-earth people with three children—two sons and a daughter. Brittany worked as an office manager, while Doug was in sales for a machine parts manufacturer. But Doug had something weighing on his mind, and before the conversation even began, he boldly puffed out his chest and declared, "I don't invest in the stock market. Never have, never will. It's worse than gambling!"

Brittany, sitting quietly beside him, lowered her gaze and shook her head. Clearly, this wasn't the first time Doug had made this proclamation.

I smiled politely and said, "I understand, Doug. But tell me, why do you feel that way?"

Doug explained, "I had a buddy at work who lost a lot of money in the market once. It's too risky."

I nodded, understanding the fear, but asked him gently, "Do you know what he invested in?"

Doug shrugged. "Some stock he read or heard about," he replied.

"I'm sorry to hear about your friend's experience," I said. "But would you mind doing a little exercise with me? I think you'll find it fun."

Doug, somewhat curious, agreed.

I asked him to walk me through his day from when he woke up. He listed the usual: "Woke up, got ready, had breakfast, went to work, ran a few errands afterward, and now I'm here."

"Great!" I said. "Now let me repeat that back to you." I began, "When you woke up this morning, you were in your house—that's real estate. You slept in a bed—furniture. You likely adjusted the thermostat—energy. You brushed your teeth, washed your hair, and put on deodorant—those are consumer staples. Brittany probably put on makeup, and you both ate breakfast—again, consumer staples. You likely took vitamins or medication—healthcare. Then you drove to work in your car—automobiles and oil. At work, you sent emails and held meetings—technology and software. After work, you used your credit or debit card to run errands—financial services."

Doug sat back, a bit surprised. "Yeah, that's about right," he admitted.

"And how many people, Doug, do you think do those same things every day, not just in America but all over the world?"

Doug thought for a moment. "A lot," he said.

"Exactly," I said. "People all over the world consume these products and services every single day, whether there's a global crisis, a change in leadership, or another wild headline in the news. These habits are ingrained in us, and they're not going anywhere. People will always brush their teeth, eat food, use energy, and rely on technology."

Here's the reality: "Consumers consume." Humans are creatures of habit. They will always brush their teeth, live in homes, eat food, use energy, rely on technology, and pay with cards. This is true not just for Doug, his family, or his neighbors but for billions of people worldwide.

I looked at Doug and said, "That's a lot of money being spent every day, isn't it?"

He nodded.

"Now," I continued, "If you were a smart investor, wouldn't it make sense to invest in the companies people rely on every day, the ones providing these everyday essentials, no matter what's happening in the world?" I continued. "Doug, what if instead of thinking of the stock market as gambling, you saw it as an opportunity to own a piece of these companies that everyone in the world is using?"

Doug's eyes widened, and a light seemed to flicker behind them. "I never thought about it like that," he said slowly. "We could make a lot of money!"

"Yes, Doug," I replied. "When you invest in a company's stock, you become part-owner of that company. When they make money, you make money. It's not gambling; it's owning a share of the companies that power the world."

At this point, Brittany smiled—a knowing, satisfied smile. "This is what I've been trying to tell you for years," she said, nudging Doug.

That day marked a turning point for Doug and Brittany. They learned that the path to building wealth is not about chasing risky trends or timing the market; it's about investing in what people will always need, want, and use. They took their first steps into investing, but not without purpose or understanding. They learned about investing in strong, reliable companies, the power of compounding returns, and the importance of staying disciplined through the market's ups and downs.

Fast-forward to today: Doug and Brittany are multimillionaires. They've achieved what I call Financial Happiness—they became Rich by Choice. And Doug? He's now one of the first clients to call me whenever the news predicts doom and gloom, excitedly saying, "Did you see the markets? Things are going to be on sale—we need to buy more!"

Investing isn't gambling—it's about understanding how people live and spend money every day. Remember, the market doesn't just reflect a series of numbers—it reflects life. And by investing in it, you're investing in the daily habits, needs, and desires of billions of people around the world.

The Core Principles of Investing: Building a Foundation for Financial Success

Welcome to a journey toward mastering the art of investing, where education meets empowerment and success is within reach. Whether you're just beginning your investment path or looking to deepen your expertise, understanding and applying a few core principles can dramatically transform your financial future. I will guide you through four fundamental components of successful investing.

To become a successful investor, you need more than just luck; you need a solid foundation built on timeless principles. Four of the most powerful are Mr. Market and Managing Your Emotions, Margin of Safety, Stick to What You Know, and Knowing What You Own and Why. These core ideas will not only guide your investment journey but also protect you from the pitfalls of emotional decision-making, uninformed choices, and short-term thinking.

1. **Mr. Market and Managing Emotions:** Investing is not just about numbers or the stock market; it's about understanding human behavior, making informed decisions, and embracing a mindset of patience and wisdom. When you learn to manage your emotions and remain calm in the face of market fluctuations (Mr. Market), you'll find yourself better equipped to make strategic decisions rather than reactive ones.

2. **Margin of Safety:** By adhering to the concept of a Margin of Safety, you'll learn to protect your investments by buying with a cushion of safety, allowing for inevitable market downturns.

3. **Stick to What You Know:** Focusing on sticking to what you know helps avoid the pitfalls of complexity and ensures you invest within your circle of competence, where you can make the most informed, confident choices.

4. **Know What You Own and Why:** One of the most overlooked aspects of investing is truly knowing what you own and why. When you understand the purpose behind each investment and how it fits into your broader strategy, you're not just a passive

participant—you're an empowered investor actively shaping your financial destiny.

My goal is to teach these principles and inspire you to approach investing with wisdom, confidence, and a clear sense of purpose. Let's dive deep into these pillars to help you become a more successful and empowered investor.

Mr. Market: The Tale of Emotion and Wealth-Building

Let me introduce you to a character who plays a role in your life every day, whether you realize it or not—Mr. Market.[74] He's everywhere. He's in your morning news, on your smartphone, and flashing across your TV screens. Some days, Mr. Market is in a fantastic mood, euphoric, driving stock prices sky-high; other days, he's despondent, and prices plummet. But here's the thing: Mr. Market isn't real. He's a fictional creation by Benjamin Graham, a legendary financial teacher and mentor to Warren Buffett, one of the wealthiest investors of all time.

Mr. Market's moods represent the stock market's daily fluctuations, swayed heavily by human emotions—fear, greed, excitement. But, as Graham once taught, "In the short run, the market is a voting machine, but in the long run, it's a weighing machine."[75] This means that while the stock price may fluctuate day-to-day based on emotional reactions, in the long term, a company's true value shines through.

Why Mr. Market's Moods Create Wealth

When the market is down, fear grips most people. But successful investors see this as the perfect opportunity. When stocks drop, it's like walking into your favorite store and seeing everything on sale. While others panic, Buffett gets excited. He knows that a temporary dip in the stock price doesn't mean the value of the company has changed. In fact, as Buffett says, "If a stock I like goes from $5 to $4, that's great news—now I can buy even more of it."[76]

Think about that. *Mr. Market's bad moods can actually help you build wealth* if you understand that value doesn't fluctuate with the emotions of the day. Great investors don't let their emotions dictate their decisions. They know that markets fluctuate based on short-term emotions, not long-term fundamentals, and they don't get discouraged by short-term downturns. They stay focused on the long-term fundamentals. "Knowledge reduces fear." When you understand how markets work, you are free to act with wisdom instead of fear.

The Real Secret: Fundamentals Over Emotions

If you view the stock market like Warren Buffett and Benjamin Graham, you'll realize that real wealth isn't found in reacting to daily news or emotional swings. The market may panic, but you don't have to. By focusing on fundamentals—the actual worth of the companies you invest in—you can weather the emotional ups and downs of Mr. Market.

Remember, the key to success is not predicting the future. It's *patience*. Templeton and Buffett made their fortunes by knowing that the real gains come from sticking with companies that are fundamentally strong, even when the market temporarily disagrees.

Embrace the Wisdom

So, next time you see the market swinging wildly, remember what Warren Buffett, John Templeton, and Benjamin Graham have taught us. Mr. Market's moods don't define you; they create opportunities. It's not about following trends or guessing the market's next move—it's about understanding that the greatest wealth is built by staying calm, focusing on value, and making smart, long-term decisions.

> **Mr. Market's moods don't define you; they create opportunities.**

> *The stock market is designed to transfer money from the Active to the Patient.*
> —Warren Buffett

The question is: Will you let Mr. Market's emotional rollercoaster scare you, or will you see it for what it truly is—a chance to buy into long-term wealth at a discount?

Margin-Of-Safety

> *Price is what you pay; value is what you get.*
> —Warren Buffett

One of Warren Buffett's favorite principles is the Margin of Safety, which is one of the cornerstones of intelligent investing. At its core, this principle means always ensuring a buffer between the price you pay for an investment and its intrinsic value. When investing, you should always leave room for error by purchasing assets well below their intrinsic value. This buffer protects investors from market volatility, miscalculations, or unforeseen events. It's like building a bridge that can support a weight far greater than you expect it to carry—this extra capacity ensures stability, even in turbulent times.

The first rule of an investment is don't lose money.
And the second rule is don't forget the first rule.
—Warren Buffett

Think of it like buying a car worth $20,000 for $15,000—that difference is your margin of safety. Or imagine you're buying a house worth $200,000. Instead of paying full price, you managed to buy it for $150,000. That $50,000 difference is your margin of safety. If the housing market dips, you still own an asset with intrinsic value, and you're less likely to lose money because you didn't pay too much upfront.

Great investors apply this concept to stocks: they seek to buy companies at a price significantly below what they believe the business is truly worth. This way, even if the market fluctuates, their investment is protected by this built-in cushion.

The margin of safety isn't about getting rich quickly; it's about avoiding unnecessary risk and ensuring long-term success. Successful investors recognize that *hope* is not a strategy. Instead, knowing that you are paying less than what something is worth provides a solid foundation for your investments, allowing for growth without being overly exposed to short-term market swings. It's a disciplined approach that transforms investing from speculation into a calculated, sustainable strategy.

Stick to What You Know: A Key to Successful Investing

An investment in knowledge pays the best interest.

—Benjamin Franklin

The greatest investors always stay within their circle of competence. They avoid the allure of flashy investments or "get rich quick" schemes because they know that lasting success comes from understanding what they own and why they own it—they never gamble on something they don't understand. "Good planning and hard work lead to prosperity, but hasty shortcuts lead to poverty," says Proverbs 21:5. Knowing the companies, industries, and markets in which you invest increases your chances of success and protects you from chasing trends that lead to disaster.

Investors like Warren Buffett have built their empires by sticking to what they know, avoiding speculation, and focusing on fundamentals. He said, "Risk comes from not knowing what you're doing."[77] When you invest in what you understand, you increase your confidence, reduce your risk, and pave the way for long-term prosperity.

Stick to What You Know is one of the most powerful investment principles and is simple yet profound. If you don't fully grasp how an investment works, its fundamentals, and why it's profitable, you shouldn't put your hard-earned money into it. Investing isn't a game of chance—it's a strategy based on knowledge, insight, and confidence in what drives the value of your holdings.

Imagine buying an investment because a coworker gave you a hot tip or because of some internet buzz. That's not a strategy; that's speculation. True investors own their investments with intention, understand the fundamentals behind them, and have a clear reason why they hold them.

Know What You Own and Why

Know what you own, and know why you own it.

—Peter Lynch

One of the most critical aspects of successful investing is having a deep understanding of what you own and why you own it. You must be fully aware of your portfolio's specific details and their role in your broader financial plan. When each investment has a clear purpose and aligns with your overall strategy, you take control of your financial future, becoming the architect of your wealth.

When you grasp not just *what* you own but the *why* behind each choice, you shift from being a passive spectator to an empowered, active participant in your financial journey. This clarity builds confidence and helps ensure that your investments work for you, not against you.

Take this example: I own dividend-growing stocks. Why? Dividend stocks provide two powerful sources of return: steady income through dividends and the potential for capital appreciation. A company that consistently raises its dividend has strong cash flow, a history of stability, and reliable performance. Over time, this dual approach adds up. The result is an investment that can outpace inflation while growing your principal.

Maybe you own an S&P 500 Index Fund. This investment doesn't require active management or stock-picking expertise. You're simply investing in the 500 largest companies in the U.S., businesses that historically grow earnings and dividends year after year. You become a part-owner of the most powerful companies in America without the headaches of running a business. *"I did nothing except buy it and leave it alone,*" and yet, you share in the profits and growth of corporate giants.

And then there are municipal bonds, like XYZ Municipal Bonds. These "Munis" offer something rare: tax-free income. Not only is the income free from federal and state taxes, but municipal bonds have an exceptionally low default rate. "Since 1970, the default rate on AAA-rated municipal bonds is less than 0.08 percent."[78] With this, you earn income without worrying about taxes, and you get peace of mind knowing your principal is likely safe.

Every investment you own should have a reason behind it. When you know *why* you own something, you gain power. This approach protects you from making the mistakes others make—buying into hype, following trends, or investing in things they don't fully understand. As Benjamin Graham once said, "The individual investor should act consistently as an investor and not as a speculator."[79]

Great investors don't rely on luck; they build their portfolios based on knowledge and insight, sticking to what they know and investing in what makes sense. Mastering this principle can protect your wealth and create a powerful path toward financial success.

Understanding the Difference Between Price and Value

Let's dig into what successful investors like Warren Buffett truly see when they look at the stock market. While many focus on stock symbols like "AAPL," Buffett and his peers see Apple Inc.—a real company with revenues, employees, products, and profits. When you buy a stock, you are not just buying a ticker symbol; you are purchasing a stake in an actual business. This business comes with overhead, cash flow, and, most importantly, the potential to generate long-term value. Successful investors don't panic when Mr. Market's mood swings wildly. The goal is to buy something for $5 when you know it's worth $10. Temporary price drops? That's an opportunity.

John Templeton, one of the greatest global stock pickers, once said, "I never ask if the market is going up or down because I don't know, and besides, it doesn't matter."[80] What mattered to him was finding undervalued companies—those priced lower than their intrinsic worth. It's not about predicting market movements; it's about focusing on value.

One of the most common mistakes people make when viewing the stock market is confusing a company's stock price with its true value. A stock price is a temporary snapshot influenced by short-term factors like market sentiment, news, or economic trends. It fluctuates daily, often driven by fear, greed, or external events that have little to do with the company's long-term potential. In contrast, a company's value is based on more stable elements, such as its fundamentals—revenues, profits, assets, and growth potential. These are the aspects that great investors focus on.

Successful investors understand this distinction and use it to their advantage. When stock prices fall below a company's intrinsic value due to market volatility, they see an opportunity to buy, knowing that the company's true worth will be recognized in the long run. Understanding the difference between price and value is key to building long-term wealth.

Meet Gary and Dorothy

Gary was the kind of man people respected before he even spoke a word. His presence alone—steady, warm, and reliable—made you feel like you were in the company of someone who knew how to navigate life's challenges. A self-made businessman, he built his reputation brick by brick through hard work and integrity. His wife, Dorothy, was his anchor, the calm to his storm of ambition. Together, they built a life centered on family, faith, and discipline, raising three wonderful children: two sons, Billy and Jordan, and their daughter, Abigail.

Gary had inherited more than just his grandfather's work ethic—he'd inherited a mindset. His grandfather's words echoed in his mind like the chorus of a familiar song: "Always save first, Gary. If you do that, you'll never go broke." So that's exactly what Gary did. Every time a new client deal came through or a promotion bumped up his pay, Gary and Dorothy had a rule—they increased their savings before anything else. As their income rose, so did their discipline. It was almost automatic. "We weren't used to that extra money anyway," Gary would say with a chuckle. "Might as well save some of it."

And they did—until they realized it wasn't working at all.

Gary and Dorothy had accumulated a small fortune in savings. On paper, it looked impressive, but their bank account told a different story. The money sat there like a ship anchored at port—steady but going nowhere. Every dollar they saved earned a fraction of a percent in interest, barely enough to buy them a cup of coffee. Meanwhile, the world outside was changing. Prices climbed higher, inflation eroded the value of their savings, and the purchasing power they thought they were building quietly slipped away like grains of sand through their fingers.

But no matter how hard they tried, their wealth wasn't growing. It felt like they were trapped in financial quicksand. With every extra hour of work, every dollar saved, and every sacrifice made, instead of rising up, they felt themselves sinking further down.

Quicksand doesn't pull you under because you're lazy. It traps you because you're fighting the wrong battle. That's what Gary and Dorothy were experiencing. Their mistake wasn't a lack of effort or discipline—it was where they were placing their trust. They had poured everything into savings accounts that earned next to nothing. Their money sat still, obedient but lifeless, unable to grow fast enough to outpace inflation. They weren't losing money—they were losing time and purchasing power, and they didn't even realize it.

It is called "Going Broke Safely."

"Going Broke Safely" is a deceptive financial trap where your money feels secure but quietly loses its power to work for you. It occurs when your savings or investments grow at a rate lower than inflation. Meaning the real value of your money shrinks over time. While you may see a steady balance or even modest gains in your account, the purchasing power of those dollars steadily erodes. In the end, you're not technically losing money, but you're losing what truly matters—your ability to afford the same lifestyle, dreams, and financial security in the future. This false sense of safety is the slow road to financial decline.

Inflation is public enemy number one. Especially for retirees, it quietly erodes the value of your hard-earned savings. It is the silent killer of wealth, making each dollar buy less over time. What seems like a comfortable nest egg today can lose its purchasing power in just a few years, leaving retirees struggling to maintain their lifestyle. Rising costs of essentials—like food, healthcare, and housing—can quickly outpace fixed incomes or low-return investments. Without proper planning and proven investment strategies, retirees risk running out of money sooner than they ever imagined.

Maybe you've felt the same way. You've been working hard, making sacrifices, doing everything "by the book," but the results aren't there. You're not lazy, and you're not careless. But, like Gary and Dorothy, you might be fighting the quicksand instead of stepping onto solid ground.

Here's the truth: Wealth isn't only built by working harder; it's built by learning to work smarter. It's built when your money becomes a teammate, not dead weight.

Gary and Dorothy learned this lesson the hard way. They were disciplined savers, but saving alone wasn't enough. They needed their money to grow, to move, to breathe. They needed to trust proven investment strategies, the kind that don't just protect you but elevate you.

Wealth isn't only built by working harder; it's built by learning to work smarter.

It was a slow-motion heartbreak. Gary was deflated, Dorothy felt stuck, and both wondered how life could be so unfair. They had done everything right—or so they thought. They budgeted carefully, lived below their means, gave generously to their church, and worked tirelessly. They were disciplined savers, but saving alone was not enough. Despite their best efforts, they couldn't seem to get ahead. Saving felt like trying to fill a leaky bucket with water. No matter how fast they worked, the bucket would never fill.

The reason, Gary later admitted, wasn't a lack of effort—it was fear. Decades earlier, he had worked for a financial firm that sent him door to door, selling families financial products they didn't need. The experience left a bitter taste in his mouth. *The firm didn't care about helping people build their future. They cared about commissions.* Gary watched as hard-working families were misled and taken advantage of. Once Gary realized what was going on, he quit, but the damage was done. A seed of distrust had been planted, and it grew like a thorny vine in his heart.

When I first met Gary, that distrust was still there, strong and thorny as ever. He wouldn't let me help him invest. And honestly, I didn't blame him. His story broke my heart, but it also made sense. Who wouldn't be skeptical after that? This same story has happened to many families. But I didn't push him. Instead, I asked for something smaller: the chance to educate him. "Let me show you the rules of investing," I told him. "Not the flashy gimmicks or quick wins, but the long-term strategies that build real wealth."

Gary reluctantly agreed, not because he was eager to invest, but because he wanted to understand. Over time, knowledge replaced fear. What once seemed risky and confusing began to make sense. He learned how to let his money grow the right way—steadily, methodically, and with discipline. Once he saw the results, something beautiful happened: Gary began to trust again.

It didn't happen overnight. We planted seeds, nurtured them, and gave them time to grow. But grow they did. Gary and Dorothy were doing just about everything right; they were only missing one final puzzle piece.

And once they did, everything changed. They stepped out of the quicksand and onto firm financial footing. The hard work they'd already put in finally had a purpose, and their savings transformed from a stagnant pond into a river of growth.

Today, Gary and Dorothy are living proof of what happens when you learn the rules of the investing game and let the power of compounding work its magic. They are multi-millionaires. The man who once feared he'd have to work forever now owns a beautiful second home on the lake, where his kids and grandkids splash in the water, roast marshmallows by the fire, and create memories that will outlast them all. Every summer, they gather there—a family bound not by financial worry but by joy.

And that's not all. Gary now takes the entire family to the beach every year, renting condos where laughter echoes off the walls and the ocean breeze carries the sound of his grandkids' giggles into the horizon. The man who once dreaded the thought of retirement now embraces it with open arms, knowing he has more than enough to live out his dreams. He's free. Financially free.

How did he get there? By trusting the process. By learning that saving alone wasn't enough. By understanding that true wealth isn't just built through hard work—it's built when your money works hard for you. Gary didn't just change his financial future. He rewrote his family's story.

Now, when Gary talks about investing, it's no longer with hesitation. It's with confidence. It's with joy. And when he looks at his grandkids running around the lake house or playing in the sand at the beach, he knows he didn't just secure his future—he secured theirs, too.

Gary and Dorothy's journey wasn't perfect, but it was powerful. And that's the truth about wealth: It's not about avoiding mistakes. It's about learning from them. It's about growth. It's about trusting the rules, trusting the process, and trusting yourself to dream bigger than you ever thought possible.

Like Gary, you can do this. You can rewrite your story, too. And when you do, the rewards aren't just measured in dollars—they're measured in memories, in freedom, and in the joy of knowing you've built a legacy that will last long after you're gone.

• • •

Great investments share a universal truth—they follow principles that stand the test of time, no matter the market. Whether it's the stock market, real estate, or acquiring businesses, the key to wealth isn't found in chasing trends but in understanding value, strategy, and long-term growth. The most successful investors don't gamble; they build. They recognize that opportunities exist everywhere—whether it's turning a distressed property into a cash-flowing asset, acquiring a business and scaling it to new heights, or compounding wealth through smart, disciplined market investments. True wealth isn't about how you invest but how well you execute—staying patient, thinking long-term, and making decisions based on wisdom, not emotion. No single path is the only way; the world is overflowing with opportunities. The secret is choosing the one that aligns with your vision, your strengths, and your ultimate goal of financial freedom.

By mastering the four principles—managing your emotions, ensuring a margin of safety, sticking to what you know, and knowing why you own something—you are laying the groundwork for a successful investment journey. Remember, it's not about getting rich quickly; it's about making thoughtful, informed decisions that lead to long-term wealth and financial freedom.

Your journey to financial happiness can start today. Even if it is 1 percent, start right now. You, too, can become a millionaire. Our goal is simple: to help you become Rich by Choice and live a life of financial happiness and freedom. You've got the power.

To explore resources from this book, scan the QR code or visit RichByChoiceBook.com/bonus.

Nick and Chelsea Master the Rules

Years ago, I wrote a heartfelt letter to my clients. A letter not just about investments but about living a life filled with peace, joy, and fulfillment. A life free from the anxiety of market fluctuations. My purpose was to illuminate a powerful truth: Market and investment turbulence is normal, predictable, and nothing to fear.

Consider this:

- **Stock Market Dip:** A short-term market decline of approximately 5%. These are frequent occurrences—averaging around three times per year—and typically represent temporary market fluctuations without long-term impact.

- **Stock Market Correction:** A decline in the market of around 10%. Corrections are relatively common, occurring slightly more than once per year on average, serving as natural adjustments within ongoing market growth.

- **Stock Market Bear Market:** Defined by a market drop of 20% or more. While these events can feel unsettling, they are less frequent, occurring about every 3 to 4 years, and are a normal, cyclical aspect of market behavior.

- **Recession:** A recession signifies a substantial and prolonged decline in economic activity, typically defined as two consecutive quarters (six months) of negative GDP growth. Historically, the U.S. has experienced a recession roughly once every five years since World War II.

In addition to the data above, I personally conducted a comprehensive analysis of every rolling 10-year period since 1900 (1900-1910, 1901-1911, 1902-1912, etc., up to 2009-2019). My research determined that, on average, approximately 3.7 out of every 10-year period experienced negative returns.

Significant Historical Market Events

- 1929: "Black Monday and Tuesday" (October 28th and 29th)
- 1934: Great Depression (Market fell 89% from peak)
- 1941: Pearl Harbor
- 1954: Dow exceeds 300, raising concerns of an overvalued market
- 1962: Cuban Missile Crisis
- 1963: JFK Assassination
- 1972: Watergate Scandal
- 1974: President Nixon resigns
- 1976: New York City threatens bankruptcy
- 1981: Assassination attempts on Ronald Reagan and Pope John Paul II
- 1987: Texaco, Inc. Bankruptcy
- 1995: Dow surpasses 4,000 and then 5,000— "Market Too High" concerns
- 1999: Y2K fears
- 2000: Dot-com bubble burst
- 2001: 9/11 terrorist attacks

- 2002: Enron Bankruptcy
- 2006: Dow surpasses 12,000—"Market Too High" concerns
- 2008: The Great Recession—the worst economic crisis since the Great Depression
- 2012: U.S. faces the "Fiscal Cliff"
- 2018: U.S.-China Trade War and fears of global economic slowdown
- 2019: Dow surpasses 28,000—"Market Too High" concerns
- 2020: COVID-19 Pandemic and Presidential Election

Even amidst a world that seems filled with constant uncertainty and alarming headlines, history has proven again and again that resilience triumphs. Despite the media's endless warnings of impending doom, the stock market has consistently risen, greatly rewarding those who remain steadfast and calm in their strategies. Our clients have done exceptionally well.

My greatest joy as your advisor isn't just witnessing your financial growth—it's seeing you live confidently, passionately, and purposefully. Worrying excessively about market fluctuations is akin to planting seeds and impatiently digging them up daily to check their growth—it's counterproductive and exhausting. Imagine investing as sailing across an ocean: storms and waves are inevitable, yet experienced sailors trust in their vessel and stay the course. Let go of worry, trust your plan, and embrace the joy of spending your days doing more of what you love with the people you love.

My ultimate hope is that you will confidently set worry aside, trusting our thoughtful strategies to guide you safely through storms and into calm waters. As you navigate life's ocean, choose to spend your precious moments creating memories, pursuing passions, and cherishing the people who mean the most to you. Remember, "Worrying is like a rocking chair—it gives you something to do but never gets you anywhere." Let your life be filled not with worry but with joyful memories, meaningful adventures, and boundless peace. After all, my wish for you is simple and heartfelt: "Do more of the things you love with the people you love."

PART III

Freedom

17

Ownership by Choice
Take Responsibility of the Small
Matters So You Can Win Big.

I n ancient times, a steward was much more than a servant—
they were the trusted managers of the noble's estate, the
ones responsible for overseeing all the day-to-day opera-
tions of the castle. The steward was, in many ways, the CEO
of the estate, entrusted with not only managing the wealth
but also expanding it, ensuring the prosperity of the household. Their mission was to protect, maintain, and maximize
all resources under their care, including relationships to live-
stock, from land to influence. Imagine walking the halls of
a grand castle, knowing every choice you make impacts not
only the present but the future generations to come. This was
the heart of stewardship.

Your goal, just like those ancient stewards, is to become the CEO of your life—*the steward of your finances, relationships, and opportunities.* The better steward you choose to become, the more you will experience Financial Happiness. And here's the beautiful part: *Anyone* can become a great steward. It doesn't require a title or royal bloodline, but rather, it demands wisdom, understanding, and a commitment to growing in every area of life. You can be Rich by Choice.

The True Meaning of Stewardship: A Holistic Approach

Stewardship goes beyond managing wealth—it's about **maximizing every aspect of life**. It's about how you spend your time, nurture your relationships, lead with love, and care for the vulnerable. You are a steward of your family, your community, your workplace, and even the resources of this planet. Great stewardship touches every corner of your existence—*from financial decisions to acts of kindness.* As Proverbs reminds us, *"Good planning and hard work lead to prosperity, but hasty shortcuts lead to poverty"* (Proverbs 21:5). In other words, being a wise steward means planning carefully, working diligently, and protecting the things that matter most.

Stewardship goes beyond managing wealth—it's about maximizing every aspect of life.

The Master and His Stewards

The biblical story of the Master and His Stewards (Matt. 25:14-30 NLT) perfectly illustrates the concept of stewardship.

> Again, the Kingdom of Heaven can be illustrated by the story of a man going on a long trip. He called his servants together and entrusted his money to them while he was gone. He gave five bags of silver to one, two bags of silver to another, and one bag of silver to the last—dividing it in proportion to their abilities. He then left on his trip.
>
> The servant who received the five bags of silver began to invest the money and earned five more. The servant with two bags of silver also went to work and earned two more. But the servant who received the one bag of silver dug a hole in the ground and hid the master's money.
>
> After a long time, their master returned from his trip and called them to give an account of how they had used his money. The servant to whom he had entrusted the five bags of silver came forward with five more and said, "Master, you gave me five bags of silver to invest, and I have earned five more."
>
> The master was full of praise. "Well done, my good and faithful servant. You have been faithful in handling this small amount, so now I will give you many more responsibilities. Let's celebrate together!"
>
> The servant who had received the two bags of silver came forward and said, "Master, you gave me two bags of silver to invest, and I have earned two more."

The master said, "Well done, my good and faithful servant. You have been faithful in handling this small amount, so now I will give you many more responsibilities. Let's celebrate together!"

Then the servant with the one bag of silver came and said, "Master, I knew you were a harsh man, harvesting crops you didn't plant and gathering crops you didn't cultivate. I was afraid I would lose your money, so I hid it in the earth. Look, here is your money back."

But the master replied, "You wicked and lazy servant! If you knew I harvested crops I didn't plant and gathered crops I didn't cultivate, why didn't you deposit my money in the bank? At least I could have gotten some interest on it."

Then he ordered, "Take the money from this servant, and give it to the one with the ten bags of silver. To those who use well what they are given, even more will be given, and they will have an abundance. But from those who do nothing, even what little they have will be taken away. Now throw this useless servant into outer darkness, where there will be weeping and gnashing of teeth."

The master entrusted his stewards with his wealth, expecting them to maximize it. One steward was given five bags of gold, another two, and another just one. The first two stewards worked diligently and doubled the wealth they were entrusted with. They took responsibility, acted with wisdom, and were praised: "Well done, good and faithful servant. You have been faithful with a few things; I will put you in charge of many things. Come, share your master's happiness" (Matt.

25:21). They had proven themselves capable of handling more because they had made the most of what they had been given.

The third steward, on the other hand, buried his single bag of gold, consumed by fear. He failed to understand the principle that stewardship is about growth, not preservation. The message is clear—those who don't take responsibility for their resources and grow them miss out on the blessings that come with true stewardship.

The Power of Responsibility and Growth

Let's put the staggering wealth in this story into perspective. The money isn't pocket change—it's life-altering wealth. In the parable, it's referred to as "bags of gold," but in the original King James Version of the Bible, they were called "talents." A talent wasn't a skill—it was a massive unit of measurement.

Throughout history, biblical scholars have used a couple of different methods to calculate money. And when biblical scholars translate its value into modern terms, the results are jaw-dropping.

One method reveals that a "talent" of gold was equivalent to 10,000 silver denarii, with one denarius representing a full day's wage for a laborer. Considering a six-day workweek, one talent represented more than 30 years of hard work. If we apply today's average American household income of $70,784, each "bag of gold" would be worth over $2 million.[81] But that's just the beginning.

Another way to calculate money is to consider the weight of a talent, which was approximately 100 pounds of gold. With gold currently trading at roughly $1,942 per ounce, this method reveals an even more stunning number—each talent would be worth over $3 million. That's the kind of money that makes your pulse quicken.

To drive this home, referring back to the original story, the first steward was entrusted with roughly $10–15 million, the second steward with $4–6 million, and even the third steward, who received the least, was given over $2–3 million. Imagine being handed that kind of responsibility. We're talking about wealth that could change your life, your children's lives, and generations beyond. This isn't just money—it's the ultimate test of stewardship and trust. What would you do if you were handed a fortune like that?

The lesson goes beyond money—it's about potential. It's about choices. Just as the stewards were given according to their abilities, so too are we. And here's the exciting part: We all have the power to *increase our ability*, to grow in wisdom, to learn, and to enhance the resources we've been given.

The call to stewardship is a call to *maximize the life you've been given*—financially, emotionally, spiritually, and relationally. As you grow in your ability to manage your resources, you will experience not only more financial success but also deeper joy, purpose, and fulfillment. After all, true stewardship is about expanding every area of your life in harmony with God's purpose for you.

Let this be your mission: to become the CEO of your own life—the choice to protect and enhance all that has been given to you.

The Power of Stewardship and Financial Happiness

Sir John Templeton once said that life's talents are not simply gifts—they are responsibilities. We are all born with the potential for greatness, but the choice is up to us to *develop and grow* those talents, not just for ourselves but for the benefit of others. Whether it's our skills, time, love, or financial resources, those who use their talents wisely, especially to help others, will be richly rewarded.

Templeton's philosophy isn't just about money—it's about becoming a steward of everything life has to offer. Money is a crucial aspect of stewardship, but it's not the only one. By developing our abilities and helping others do the same, we create a ripple effect of generosity and kindness in the world. As you grow in your financial knowledge and practice wise stewardship, the blessings multiply—not only for you but for everyone you touch.

The Problem with Sudden Wealth

Most people dream of sudden riches, believing a lottery jackpot or an unexpected windfall will solve all their problems. But wealth isn't just about money—it's about the person managing it. If you aren't prepared to handle wealth with wisdom, discipline, and integrity, that money won't bring you happiness—it will bring you stress, chaos, and regret.

Did you know that most lottery winners don't end up living happily ever after? In fact, studies show that 80 percent of them experience negative consequences, and 70 percent go bankrupt within just seven years.[82] Why? Because money can be an incredible blessing or a pain-ridden curse. Wealth without preparation is a burden, not a blessing.

> **Wealth isn't just about money—it's about the person managing it.**

Jack Whittaker

In 2002, Jack Whittaker, a West Virginia businessman, won $315 million in the Powerball jackpot.[83] It was the largest single-ticket payout at the time. Whittaker vowed to use the money for good, pledging to donate millions to charity. But what started as a dream turned into a devastating nightmare.

Whittaker's life spiraled as his newfound fortune attracted unwanted attention. He became a target for lawsuits, theft, and con artists. His home was repeatedly broken into, and over $545,000 in cash was stolen from his car on two separate occasions.

The most tragic fallout came within his family. His granddaughter, Brandi, whom he adored and spoiled with gifts, developed a severe drug addiction fueled by the sudden access to wealth. In 2004, her boyfriend died of an overdose in Whittaker's home, and a few months later, Brandi herself was found dead, wrapped in plastic and dumped behind a van.

Whittaker fell into depression and heavy drinking, his marriage crumbled, and his life was ruined. Reflecting on the curse of his winnings, he admitted, "I wish I'd torn that ticket up."

We see this not just in lottery winners but also in professional athletes who go from earning millions to financial ruin in just a few years. Nearly 80 percent of retired NFL players face financial stress within two years of leaving the league, and 60 percent of former NBA players are broke within five years.[84] These are individuals who had been given more than enough money to build generational wealth, yet they lost it all. Not because they weren't talented, but because they weren't financially prepared.

A Lesson in Becoming the Person Who Can Handle Wealth

Money doesn't change who you are; it magnifies who you are. If you're irresponsible with $1,000, you'll be irresponsible with $1 million. If you lack education and discipline with a small income, you'll lack it with a fortune. This is why true financial success isn't about luck—it's about *who you become.*

The ultimate goal in life isn't just to have or even to do. Your first goal is to become. Become the person capable of creating, sustaining, and growing it. Think of it like a magnet—the stronger you are in character, discipline, and wisdom, the more wealth and success you will naturally attract. I wish for you to become a great CEO of your life.

Money doesn't change who you are; it magnifies who you are.

It's not about hoping money falls into your lap; it's about building the internal strength to handle and multiply it when it does. True financial happiness isn't found in sudden riches—it's found in becoming the person who can create and sustain wealth, not just for yourself but for those around you.

- Are your daily choices aligned with the life you want to have?

- Are you the kind of person today who can handle the life you dream of tomorrow?

- Are you currently the person you need to be in order to live the life of your dreams?

- Right now, are your daily habits building the future you want, or are they keeping you stuck in the past?

- If your current actions were multiplied over the next five years, would they lead you to wealth—or regret?

- Would your future self thank you for the decisions you're making today?

- Are you truly in control of your financial future, or are you just hoping for the best?

Be honest with yourself. I want to inspire you to take action.

If we want to receive more in life, we must first prove that we can handle what we already have. Why would we be entrusted with more if we are careless with the little? As Proverbs 4:7 reminds us, "The beginning of wisdom is this: Get wisdom. Though it cost all you have, get understanding." Wisdom is the foundation of great stewardship. Learn, grow, and be prepared for the blessings to come.

Imagine a modern version of the ancient story of the Master of the Castle and his stewards. In today's world, this would be akin to a business owner hiring three different CEOs to lead three different companies. Each CEO is entrusted with the company's future, and much like the stewards, the more capable and proven the CEO, the larger and more successful the company they are given to manage. Wouldn't you, as the owner, choose to place your most skilled and talented CEO in charge of your biggest and most valuable enterprise?

As Harvard Business School defines it, the role of a CEO is to make major corporate decisions, oversee resources, and drive the company's growth through high-level strategic planning.[85] Ultimately, a CEO is responsible for the success or failure of the organization. Now, think of yourself as the *CEO of your life and finances.* You have the incredible opportunity to improve not only your family's financial future but also the quality of life for everyone you love. You are entrusted with the responsibility of stewarding your resources—*time, money, and talent*—to create long-term success.

Great CEOs make decisions that impact not only the company but also the lives of their employees. In the same way, your choices around money management and financial growth can transform the future for your family.

> *Someone's sitting in the shade today because*
> *someone planted a tree a long time ago.*
> —Warren Buffett

The more you grow your ability to manage your finances with wisdom and intention, the more you'll be blessed, and the greater impact you'll have on the lives of those you care about. Embrace the role of CEO in your life and unlock the path to greater success, becoming Rich by Choice and Financial Happiness.

To explore resources from this book, scan the QR code or visit RichByChoiceBook.com/bonus.

Nick and Chelsea Embracing Ownership

Thoughts from Nick and Chelsea on Embracing Ownership

Imagine walking through the halls of your life like the steward of a grand castle—every step echoing with purpose, every decision shaping your family's legacy. That's the power of ownership. It's not about control—it's about care. It's about being entrusted with something sacred: your time, your money, your relationships, your future. Ownership is choosing to stop waiting for someone else to fix things or make things happen. It's rising each day and saying, *"I am the CEO of my life."* And just like a wise CEO, we must act with vision, humility, and relentless intention.

The truth is, God has already placed incredible resources in your hands—some visible, some still unfolding. Whether it's $100 or $100,000, a small circle or a large platform, what you do with what you've been given matters. Ownership doesn't begin when you "have more"; it begins when you recognize the value of what's already yours and multiply it.

We all have the ability to grow, to rise, to lead—starting now. Ownership isn't a title. It's a decision. It's a choice. And when you embrace it fully, you unlock a life of impact, purpose, and true Financial Happiness.

Ownership into Action:
Three Simple Habits That Ignite Massive Progress

1. **Think in 3s.**

   Don't overwhelm yourself with a 20-item to-do list. Instead, follow the rule of 3: Set three bold goals per quarter, three weekly priorities, and three daily tasks. These micro-wins create macro-results. Focus drives achievement; distraction kills it.

2. **Master Single-Tasking.**

   Multitasking is a myth—it's just mental ping-pong. Choose one meaningful task and go all-in. Eliminate distractions. Use tools like website blockers to guard your focus. Every time you switch gears, you lose momentum. Instead, lock in and let progress snowball.

3. **Build Accountability & Momentum.**

   Track your wins. Note your obstacles. Reflect, don't regret. Apps and journals can help, but community fuels growth. Join a mastermind or accountability group—surround yourself with others chasing greatness. The energy will lift you higher. Shared goals spark extraordinary effort.

Final Thoughts

Positive thinking sets the stage, and *positive action* brings the curtain up. Own your goals. Align your mind. Take deliberate, focused steps—and watch the life you imagine become the life you live. We are so excited for you and want to hear all about your journey and how great your life has become. Please email us your success story so we can celebrate with you.

18

Rich by Choice
Your Path to an
Extraordinary Life.

Reflecting on my life, I can see how every hardship, every success, and every lesson prepared me for the life I'm living now. My parents' divorce showed me the devastating impact financial struggle can have on a family. Basketball taught me the power of discipline and small, consistent actions. My internship and mentors revealed the importance of integrity and always putting others first. The life-altering sermon at church opened my eyes to the deeper purpose behind wealth. My mentors inspired me to become better, showing me the need to passionately pursue education, and by becoming better, I can have a greater positive impact on the families we serve. Then, at a crossroads in my life, I gratefully learned the power of my wife and I working together as one.

I am forever grateful for these experiences, for they have shaped the person I am today. They taught me that wealth isn't just about accumulating money; it's about using it as a tool to create freedom, security, and happiness. My mission is clear: take everything I've learned—through my education, business experience, and personal journey—and share it with you. I've seen firsthand the secrets to building real wealth and happiness, and I'm here to show you the proven process. It's not about a quick fix or a magic formula. It's about mastering the Fundamentals of Money and breaking through the barriers that hold so many people back. You can be Rich by Choice, and it starts right now.

My Hope for You

Imagine the potential within 100 people starting at the same point in life, all at the age of 25, filled with hopes, dreams, and excitement about their futures. According to the timeless insights of Earl Nightingale in *The Strangest Secret*, every one of them believes they are destined for success. You can see it in their eyes—the sparkle, the eagerness, the excitement for life's adventure. But by the time they reach 65, only one will be rich, and just five will have achieved financial independence. The remaining 95 will still struggle, either broke or working endlessly with their dreams left behind.

What happens to that spark, to their dreams? Nightingale's message is just as relevant today as in the 1950s, but only a small percentage of people reach true success. *Why?*

The answer lies in financial literacy and intentional action. Success isn't just about wealth—it's about financial happiness, where you live a life free from money stress, health concerns from financial worry, and the anxiety of an uncertain future. But here's the exciting part—it doesn't have to be this way for you.

In America, a land overflowing with opportunity, the only thing standing between you and financial freedom is your commitment to learning. "The purpose of human life is to serve and show compassion and the will to help others," said Albert Schweitzer.[86] This book serves to grow the 5.8 percent of those who achieve financial success. The proven principles of money are within your reach; now is the time to harness them.

Why not you? Why can't you be the one who breaks free from the financial struggles and joins the small percentage who experience financial peace and freedom? The answer is—you can! You will transform your life by understanding these principles, embracing financial education, and acting with purpose. Earl Nightingale said, "You become what you think about," so start thinking about success and decide to pursue it today.[87]

Carpe Diem: Seize the day.

In *Dead Poets Society*, Robin Williams plays an unconventional teacher who challenges his students to think differently—to live differently. One day, he takes his class to the hallway, where old black-and-white photos of students from over a century ago hang on the walls. He tells them to look at those faces closely:

> They're not that different from you, are they? Same haircuts. Full of hormones, just like you. Invincible, just like

you feel. The world is their oyster. They believe they're destined for great things, just like many of you. Their eyes are full of hope, just like you. Did they wait until it was too late to make from their lives even one iota of what they were capable of? Because, you see, gentlemen, these boys are now fertilizing daffodils. But if you listen real close, you can hear them whisper their legacy to you. Go on, lean in. Listen, you hear it? – Carpe. – Hear it? – Carpe. Carpe diem. Seize the day, boys. Make your lives extraordinary.[88]

Seize the day. Life is short. The Bible tells us in James 4:14, "Your life is like the morning fog; it's here a little while, then it's gone." There's no time to waste. Don't wait for the "right time" or until you feel "ready." The power to transform your life is in your hands right now.

My hope for you is more than survival, getting by, and just having a decent or okay life. No! You should demand more. Life isn't meant to be lived in mediocrity or boredom. It's meant to be an adventure, one that gets better and more exciting as the days go by.

You have within you the capacity to achieve incredible success, not just financially but in every aspect of life. I want you to experience what it means to be Rich by Choice: a life overflowing with love, laughter, peace, joy, adventure, freedom, and fulfillment. You and your family deserve that kind of life.

Don't wait another second. It's never too late. Whether you're 25 or 75, your capacity to build wealth and create lasting happiness is far greater than you might think. Franklin, Lincoln, Carnegie, and Hill understood that the prime years to build financial success are ages 40 to 70. That's a vast window of opportunity!

You are never too young, never too old to begin. "One today is worth two tomorrows."[89] Start right now. Take bold action toward that extraordinary life you've always dreamed of—a life of being Rich by Choice.

The only moment you truly have is now. Seize it. Make your life extraordinary. Time is finite. Every day is a gift. Every moment you let slip away is a moment lost from the life you could be living. Imagine what could have been—don't let your future be filled with regret.

Action is the key that unlocks the door to the life you crave. Think about that for a moment. Knowledge is just potential energy waiting to be unleashed. Your daily actions are the brushstrokes that paint the masterpiece of your future. Your daily actions form your habits, and, in turn, your habits sculpt and shape your destiny.

Live by the Fundamentals of Money. They will lead you to a life beyond your wildest dreams. You'll experience more Financial Happiness than you ever thought possible—a life filled with peace, prosperity, and freedom.

Those daily disciplines, those small yet significant actions, will compound over time, creating a life that's rich not only in wealth but in purpose, meaning, and joy.

Visualize your future self thriving. A life where you have the financial security to live your dreams, provide for your family, and give generously. Picture yourself waking up every morning with a deep sense of gratitude and excitement for the day ahead because you know you've taken the steps to craft the life you deserve.

Time waits for no one. The life you've always wanted is on the other side of action. It's within your grasp. But you must reach out and take it. Seize this moment, and commit to living a life of action, a life of power, and a life of Financial Happiness.

Yesterday is gone, and tomorrow isn't promised. But today is the gift you've been waiting for—it's the tomorrow you've been longing for, right here in your hands. The power to change your life is already within you. It's there, waiting to be unleashed.

I want you to remember this always: You are worth it. Your life, dreams, and loved ones are all worth every ounce of energy and effort you invest. When I talk about "wealth," "riches," or "Financial Happiness," I'm not just speaking about money. Yes, money is part of the equation, but these words symbolize so much more. They are metaphors for living your most extraordinary life, becoming the best version of yourself, and creating a life filled with happiness, love, and fulfillment.

I want you to experience the kind of wealth that isn't just about numbers in a bank account—it's about million-dollar memories. Imagine traveling the world, making priceless memories on incredible vacations, and having grand adventures with the people you love. Picture a life where you are rich in peace, overflowing with laughter, and surrounded by the warmth of a united, loving family. That's the wealth I want for you. A wealth that makes you smile from the depths of your soul. A life that gives you a million moments that take your breath away, a million hugs from your precious children and grandchildren, and a million reasons to be thankful every single day.

To reach that place of abundance, you must first take action. Read, learn, and apply the lessons in this book to your life. Decide—right now—what you want from life, what will bring you joy, and what your ideal future looks like. Then, begin immediately from where you stand today. Yesterday is gone forever. Tomorrow may never arrive, but today is yesterday's tomorrow within your hands.

God bless you on your journey to becoming Rich by Choice. I will be praying for you. Go forward with courage, and may your life be filled with an abundance of love, peace, security, becoming Rich by Choice, and... FINANCIAL HAPPINESS!

To explore resources from this book, scan the QR code or visit RichByChoiceBook.com/bonuses.

Endnotes

1   Jim Kwik, *Limitless* (New York, NY: Hay House LLC, 2020).
2   Jason Selk and Ellen Reed, *Relentless Solution Focus: Train Your Mind to Conquer Stress, Pressure, and Underperformance* (New York, NY: McGraw Hill, 2021).
3   Henry David Thoreau and Walter Harding, *Walden: An Annotated Edition* (Boston, MA: Houghton Mifflin, 1995).
4   Alexandria White, "90% of Americans Say Money Impacts Their Stress Level, According to Survey," CNBC, May 1, 2024, https://www.cnbc.com/select/why-americans-are-stressed-about-money/.
5   Ibid
6   Sophie Bethune and Angel Brownawell, "APA Survey Shows Money Stress Weighing on Americans' Health Nationwide," American Psychological Association, 2015, https://www.apa.org/news/press/releases/2015/02/money-stress.
7   "Money on Your Mind," Money and Mental Health, June 2016, https://www.moneyandmentalhealth.org/wp-content/uploads/2016/06/Money-on-your-mind-full-report.pdf.
8   "Planning & Progress Study 2018," Northwestern Mutual, 2018, https://news.northwesternmutual.com/planning-and-progress-2018.
9   Lawrence Robinson and Melinda Smith, "Coping with Financial Stress," HelpGuide.org, July 31, 2024, https://www.helpguide.org/mental-health/stress/coping-with-financial-stress.

10 Sharon Feiereisen, "The 12 Biggest Money-Related
    Reasons People Get Divorced," Business Insider,
    July 7, 2019, https://www.businessinsider.com/
    divorce-money-issues-financial-relationship-couple-2019-7.
11 Ramsey Solutions, "Money Ruining Marriages in America:
    A Ramsey Solutions Study," Ramsey Solutions, February
    7, 2018, https://www.ramseysolutions.com/company/
    newsroom/releases/money-ruining-marriages-in-america.
12 Ramsey Solutions, "Money, Marriage, and
    Communication," Ramsey Solutions, September 27,
    2021, https://www.ramseysolutions.com/relationships/
    money-marriage-communication-research.
13 "2019 Modern Wealth Survey," Schwab Brokerage, February
    17, 2019, https://www.aboutschwab.com/modernwealth2019.
14 Ramsey Solutions, "Money, Marriage, and Communication."
15 "With This Ring: A National Survey on Marriage
    in America," With This Ring: A National Survey on
    Marriage in America, 2005, https://www.fatherhood.org/
    with-this-ring-survey.
16 Kelly Kenneally, "New Report: 40% of Older
    Americans Rely Solely on Social Security for
    Retirement Income," National Institute on Retirement
    Security, January 14, 2020, https://www.nirsonline.
    org/2020/01/new-report-40-of-older-american
    s-rely-solely-on-social-security-for-retirement-income/.
17 Ibid.
18 Scot Anderson, *Think like a Billionaire, Become a Billionaire:
    As a Man Thinks, so Is He* (Tulsa, OK: Harrison House,
    2012).
19 Katie Brockman, "40% of Americans Expect
    to Keep Working in Retirement. Is That Right
    for You?," USA Today, June 4, 2020, https://
    eu.usatoday.com/story/money/2020/06/04/
    americans-keep-working-retirement-is-that-
    right/111896160/.

20   Andrea Woroch, "18 Surprising Personal Finance Statistics (2025)," BadCredit.org, July 31, 2023, https://www.badcredit.org/how-to/personal-finance-statistics/.

21   Tom Anderson, "81% of Americans Don't Know How Much They Need to Retire," CNBC, February 15, 2017, https://www.cnbc.com/2017/02/15/80-of-americans-dont-know-how-much-they-need-to-retire.html.

22   Christo Petrov, "20+ Incredible Personal Finance Statistics to Know in 2025," Spendmenot, July 22, 2024, https://spendmenot.com/personal-finance-statistics/.

23   Ibid.

24   Ibid.

25   Rachel Lustbader, "2020 Estate Planning and Wills Study," Caring, February 21, 2025, https://www.caring.com/caregivers/estate-planning/wills-survey/2020-survey/.

26   Petrov.

27   Northwestern Mutual.

28   Ashlea Ebeling, "Billions in 401(k) Match Dollars Unclaimed," Forbes, May 12, 2015, https://www.forbes.com/sites/ashleaebeling/2015/05/12/billions-in-401k-match-dollars-unclaimed/?sh=3bcef37b2791.

29   Sean Dennison, "64% of Americans Aren't Prepared for Retirement - and 48% Don't Care," GOBankingRates, September 23, 2019, https://www.gobankingrates.com/retirement/planning/why-americans-will-retire-broke/.

30   Petrov.

31   Schwab Brokerage.

32   Katharina Buchholz, "Chart: One Third of Americans Have More Credit Debt than Savings | Statista," Statista, February 14, 2019, https://www.statista.com/chart/17018/more-credit-card-debt-than-savings-us/.

33   Alexandria White, "Americans Have an Average of 4 Credit Cards-Is That Too Many?," CNBC, November 13, 2024, https://www.cnbc.com/select/how-many-credit-cards-does-the-average-american-have/.

34 Ibid.

35 Sarah O'Brien, "Consumers Paying $104 Billion in Credit Card Interest and Fees," CNBC, July 20, 2018, https://www.cnbc.com/2018/07/19/consumers-paying-104-billion-in-credit-card-interest-and-fees.html.

36 Petrov.

37 Woroch

38 Julia Falcon, "Even with Mortgage Assistance, 47% of Homeowners Have Considered Selling Their Home Due to Pandemic," HousingWire, June 18, 2020, https://www.housingwire.com/articles/even-with-mortgage-assistance-47-of-homeowners-have-considered-selling-their-home-due-to-pandemic/.

39 Meg Moyer, "Understanding Family Financial Capability," Financial Capability Network, February 2018, https://everfi.com/wp-content/uploads/2018/02/FamilyFinancialCapability_Whitepaper-1.pdf.

40 Madeline Farber, "Nearly Two-Thirds of Americans Can't Pass a Basic Test of Financial Literacy," Fortune, July 12, 2016, https://fortune.com/2016/07/12/financial-literacy/.

41 Robert Puff, "The Pitfalls to Pursuing Happiness," Psychology Today, September 19, 2018, https://www.psychologytoday.com/us/blog/meditation-modern-life/201809/the-pitfalls-pursuing-happiness.

42 Sonja Lyubomirsky, Kennon M. Sheldon, and David Schkade, "Pursuing Happiness: The Architecture of Sustainable Change," *Review of General Psychology* 9, no. 2 (June 2005): 111–31, https://doi.org/10.1037/1089-2680.9.2.111.

43 Barbara L. Fredrickson, "The Role of Positive Emotions in Positive Psychology: The Broaden-and-Build Theory of Positive Emotions.," *American Psychologist* 56, no. 3 (2001): 218–26, https://doi.org/10.1037//0003-066x.56.3.218.

44 Napoleon Hill, *Think and Grow Rich: Original 1937 Edition* (Duke Classics, 2012).

45 Viktor E. Frankl, *Man's Search for Meaning* (Boston, MA: Beacon Press Books, 2017).

46 Kidal Delonix, "The Harvard MBA Study on Goal Setting," Quantum Books, July 24, 2018, https://www.quantumbooks.com/home-and-family/personal-development/the-harvard-mba-study-on-goal-setting.

47 Jeff Bollow, "How Fast Is Your Brain?," How Fast is Your Brain? | The Phenomenal Experience, accessed February 28, 2025, https://thephenomenalexperience.com/content/how-fast-is-your-brain.

48 "What Is the Memory Capacity of a Human Brain?," Clinical Neurology Specialists, February 1, 2024, https://www.cnsnevada.com/what-is-the-memory-capacity-of-a-human-brain/.

49 Eric Lai, "Size Matters: Yahoo Claims 2-Petabyte Database Is World's Biggest, Busiest," Computerworld, May 22, 2008, https://www.computerworld.com/article/1564841/size-matters-yahoo-claims-2-petabyte-database-is-world-s-biggest-busiest.html.

50 Kwik.

51 Bollow.

52 Emily Kwong, "Understanding Unconscious Bias," NPR, July 15, 2020, https://www.npr.org/2020/07/14/891140598/understanding-unconscious-bias?utm_source=chatgpt.com.

53 James Allen, *As a Man Thinketh* (Chicago, IL: Prakash Books, 2023).

54 John Templeton, *Worldwide Laws of Life: 200 Eternal Spiritual Principles* (West Conshohocken, PA: Templeton Foundation Press, 2011).

55 Allen.

56 Henry Ford and Samuel Crowther, My Life and Work (Duke Classics, 2024).

57 Earl Nightingale, *The Strangest Secret* (Chicago, IL: Nightingale-Conant Corp. : Distributed by Dartnell Corp, 1970).

58 Allen.

59 Albert Einstein, "A Quote by Albert Einstein," Goodreads, accessed February 28, 2025, https://www.goodreads.com/quotes/38836-imagination-is-everything-it-is-the-preview-of-life-s-coming?utm_source=chatgpt.com.

60 Hill.

61 Andrew Carnegie and David Nasaw, *The "Gospel of Wealth" Essays and Other Writings Andrew Carnegie* (New York, NY: Penguin Books, 2006).

62 Plato, *The Symposium: Walter Hamilton Edition* (London, UK: Penguin Classics, 1995).

63 John Templeton and James Whitfield Ellison, *The Templeton Plan: 21 Steps to Success and Happiness* (West Conshohocken, Pa, PA: Templeton Press, 2013).

64 Neil Shah, "For Many U.S. Families, Financial Disaster Is Just One Setback Away - WSJ," For Many U.S. Families, Financial Disaster Is Just One Setback Away, January 29, 2015, https://www.wsj.com/articles/BL-REB-30418.

65 Robert T. Kiyosaki, *Rich Dad Poor Dad* (Scottsdale, AZ: Plata Publishing, 2022).

66 Ramsey Solutions, "The State of Debt among Americans," Ramsey Solutions, September 24, 2021, https://www.ramseysolutions.com/debt/state-of-debt-among-americans-research?srsltid=AfmBOooboaVnJOz8iE0GU435Qc7iLjq0YftKq7j3h1pMHdxMzJkEQ62P.

67 Warren Buffett and Lawrence A. Cunningham, *The Essays of Warren Buffett: Lessons for Corporate America* (New York, NY: Cunningham Group, 2023).

68 Dave Ramsey, The Total Money Makeover: A Proven Plan for Financial Peace (Nashville, TN: Thomas Nelson Publishing, 2024).

69 Kiyosaki.

70 Eric Jorgenson, *The Almanack of Naval Ravikant* (BookBaby, 2020).

71 This story was inspired by Jeff Olson's *The Slight Edge*. [Jeff Olson, *The Slight Edge* (McMahons Point, Sydney, Australia: Goko Publishing, 2016).]

72 Adam Hayes, "5 Simple Investing Moves Warren Buffett Has Used to Become a Billionaire," Investopedia, January 26, 2025, https://www.investopedia.com/simple-warren-buffett-investing-moves-8778968.

73 Charles T. Munger et al., *Poor Charlie's Almanack: The Essential Wit and Wisdom of Charles T. Munger* (South San Francisco, CA, CA: Stripe Press, 2023).

74 Benjamin Graham, *The Intelligent Investor* (New York, NY: Harper Business, 2006).

75 Ibid.

76 "Buffett's Timeless Advice When Stocks Are Falling," CNBC, September 16, 2022, https://link.cnbc.com/public/29081083.

77 Buffett and Cunningham.

78 Nick Murray, *Simple Wealth, Inevitable Wealth* (Southold, NY: Nick Murray Company, Inc, 2019).

79 Graham.

80 Templeton.

81 Jessica Semega and Melissa Kollar, "Income in the United States: 2021," Census.gov, September 13, 2022, https://www.census.gov/library/publications/2022/demo/p60-276.html.

82 "Research Statistic on Financial Windfalls and Bankruptcy," NEFE, January 12, 2018, https://www.nefe.org/news/2018/01/research-statistic-on-financial-windfalls-and-bankruptcy.aspx.

83 "Jack Whittaker (Lottery Winner)," Wikipedia, January 22, 2025, https://en.wikipedia.org/wiki/Jack_Whittaker_(lottery_winner)#:~:text=Andrew%20Jackson%20Whittaker%20Jr.&text=His%20win%20of%20US%24314.9,and%20experienced%20several%20personal%20tragedies.

84   Pablo S. Torre, "How (and Why) Athletes Go Broke - Sports Illustrated Vault," SI.com, March 23, 2009, https://vault. si.com/vault/2009/03/23/how-and-why-athletes-go-broke.

85   Hubert Joly, "Infusing the Organization with Purpose Can Drive Extraordinary Results: Executive Education," Harvard Business School, October 16, 2024, https://www.exed.hbs.edu/blog/ infusing-organization-purpose-can-drive-extraordinary-results.

86   Albert Schweitzer, *My Life and Thought: An Autobiography* (London, UK: Allen & Unwin, 1966).

87   Earl Nightingale, *The Strangest Secret* (Chicago, IL: Nightingale-Conant Corp. : Distributed by Dartnell Corp, 1970).

88   *Dead Poets Society*, film (United States: Touchstone, Distributed by Image Entertainment, 1989).

89   Nightingale.

Acknowledgments

I would be remiss if I did not acknowledge my mom, dad, brothers, and my children, Daegen Knox, Kinsley Blayke, Nicholas Brooks, and Everly Le'Ann. Your unwavering support and love have always been a source of inspiration and comfort through this journey called life.

I would also (most importantly) like to thank my amazing wife, Chelsea. Your countless and selfless sacrifices have been great through this difficult process. Thank you. Emphatically, you are the most incredible person I have ever met. You are my reason, "Why"! I am incredibly grateful and thank God every day for bringing our lives together. Everything amazing in my life begins and ends with you. My love for you is unwavering, and because of you, I am filled with gratitude and excitement about the amazing adventure of our future together.

About the Author

Dr. Nicholas E. Michels is a trusted guide, teacher, public speaker, and bestselling author whose passion lies in empowering people to live rich, fulfilling lives—not just financially, but in joy, love, and purpose. With a career spanning three different decades, Nick has helped thousands eliminate stress, build wealth, and create a legacy through his proven Elite Wealth Management Process.

Rich By Choice is a powerful reminder that you hold the ability to shape your destiny, choosing to be rich in peace, joy, and fulfillment while creating the life you've always dreamed of. Dr. Nicholas E. Michels takes you on an inspiring journey, equipping you with the tools and strategies to make the right choices and unlock a life of abundance, purpose, and happiness.

As the founder of Michels Family Financial, Nick is a CERTIFIED FINANCIAL PLANNER™, CERTIFIED PRIVATE WEALTH ADVISOR™, Licensed Money Manager, and National Social Security Advisor, and holds a

Doctorate in Business Administration. His mission is clear: to transform how people view and use money, helping them make smarter financial decisions that lead to peace, security, and an amazing life of happiness. His approach is rooted in education and relationships, ensuring that his clients feel empowered to achieve their dreams.

Nick's journey began in both abundance and hardship, an experience that taught him early on the profound influence money has on life and relationships. His first-class education in psychology and finance, combined with his time as a professional athlete, gave him the tools to serve others with clarity, confidence, and compassion. A two-time first-team All-American and Academic All-American basketball player at Dallas Baptist University, Nick went on to travel the world with Athletes in Action, where he learned the value of pursuing passion and serving others.

Nick's bestselling book, *Rich By Choice*, captures his mission to help people reframe their relationship with money. More than just a financial guide, it's an invitation to embrace a life rich in relationships, laughter, and meaning while building financial security and legacy. His philosophy is simple yet profound: Money is a tool to enhance your life, not define it.

Outside his work, Nick is a devoted husband to his wife, Chelsea, and a proud father to their three children, Daegen, Kinsley, and Brooks. Together, Nick and Chelsea are deeply committed to giving back through The Michels Corporation, their charitable foundation that supports youth education, families in need, global missions, and causes close to their hearts. Whether coaching clients, writing, or serving in his community, Nick's life's work is a testament to the power of generosity, gratitude, and purpose.

Unlock the Secrets to Financial Success!

You've begun your journey with Rich by Choice, but the path to financial happiness doesn't stop here. Connect with our exclusive community to receive ongoing education, powerful insights, and actionable strategies that will help you and your family thrive. Access articles, videos, live Q&A sessions, and more—everything you need to make informed and inspired financial decisions.

UNLOCK EXCLUSIVE INSIGHTS AND STRATEGIES TO SUPERCHARGE YOUR JOURNEY TO FINANCIAL HAPPINESS TODAY!

Are You Truly Rich by Choice?

Discover how aligned your financial choices are with your life goals and values through the exclusive Rich by Choice Assessment. In less than 10 minutes, you'll gain profound insights into your financial strengths, uncover areas for growth, and receive customized guidance to elevate your financial happiness.

"Ready to be Rich by Choice?

Scan here to unlock your personal path to Financial Happiness now!"

DON'T GUESS—ASSESS!

Empowering Future Generations Through Money Education

The Michels Family Corporation is committed to transforming lives by teaching kids essential financial principles.

From budgeting basics and savvy savings to the magic of compounding interest, we equip children with the skills they need for lifelong financial happiness. Our engaging seminars, workshops, and community initiatives are offered FREE of charge.